Bauhaus Archive Berlin   The collection

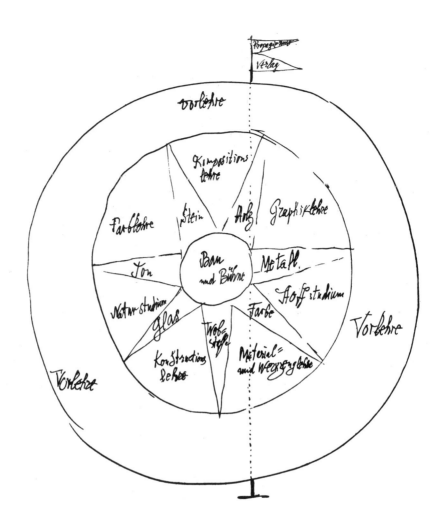

Paul Klee
Idea and structure
of the State
Bauhaus, 1922
Pen drawing
Acquired through
the Federal
Ministry of the
Interior and the
Land Berlin

Bauhaus Archive Berlin
Museumspädagogischer
Dienst Berlin

Berlin 2004

Bauhaus Archive Berlin

Museum of Design

The collection

Published by
Bauhaus Archive Berlin
Museumspädagogischer Dienst Berlin

Texts
Magdalena Droste (MD)
Peter Hahn (PH)
Karsten Hinz (KH)
Klaus Weber (KW)
Christian Wolsdorff (CW)

Illustrations
Sabine Hartmann

Translation
Helen Adkins

Editing
Andrea Scrima
Richard Carpenter
Elisabeth Moortgat (MD Berlin)

Graphic design
Georg von Wilcken (MD Berlin)
Marc Mendelson

Production
H. Heenemann GmbH & Co, Berlin

© 2004
Bauhaus Archive Berlin
Klingelhöferstraße 14
D-10785 Berlin

Die Deutsche Bibliothek-CIP-Einheitsaufnahme
Bauhaus-Archiv <Berlin>:
Bauhaus Archive Berlin : Museum of Design,
the collection / Bauhaus Archive Berlin ;
Museumpädagogischer Dienst Berlin.
[Texte Magdalena Droste … Red. Elisabeth
Moortgat. Aus dem Dt. von Helen Adkins]. -
Berlin : Museumspädag. Dienst, 1999
Dt. Ausg. u.d.T. : Bauhaus-Archiv <Berlin>:
Bauhaus-Archiv Berlin
ISBN 3-930929-10-4

Contents

Foreword and acknowledgements

When in 1960 the Bauhaus Archive was founded as a non-profit association, the goal was set to collect all »documents related to the activities and cultural philosophy of the Bauhaus« and make these accessible to the public. Here, the concern is not only for documents in a narrower sense – written records such as letters, manuscripts, files etc. – but most importantly for the artistic production of teachers and students in the fields of graphic arts, painting, architecture, photography, and design. Now, after 45 years of committed collecting, the Bauhaus Archive owns the worldwide largest collection on the theme of the Bauhaus.

The point of departure for the assembly of such a collection was by no means easy. Indeed, in postwar Germany not nearly as much importance was attached to the Bauhaus – founded in 1919 and closed in 1933 under the pressure of National Socialists – as is given today to this most significant art school of the 20th century. In addition, no cohesive archival collection from the Bauhaus that could have formed a base for the holdings had been preserved. And the major centers of activity of the school – Weimar and Dessau – were located in the GDR, where the Bauhaus was regarded to be bourgeois and formalistic and where access to existing files was seriously restricted.

With the support of the Bauhaus masters, most of whom had to leave Germany after 1933, and of many former students, Hans Maria Wingler, founder and first director of the Bauhaus Archive, began building up the collection. Walter Gropius laid the foundations by donating his vast personal archive on the Bauhaus, in addition to which he also supplied the design for an adequate building. This was to open in 1979 in Berlin, where the Bauhaus Archive had by then moved to, hence carrying the subtitle »Museum of Design«. The building with its striking shed roof silhouette was listed in 1997 and belongs today to the architectural sights of the German capital.

Here the visitor encounters all the phases of activity and locations of the Bauhaus through a surprising variety of works executed in all the media of the arts during the few years of institutional existence between 1919 and 1933: from the initial Expressionist inclination in Weimar, to the increasingly objective orientation and establishment as school of design in Dessau, and to the remodeling as a school of architecture in Berlin.

Such a rich collection could never have come together without the support of the members of the Bauhaus and their families. We thank them and all our patrons, first of all the Land Berlin, that covers not only our running costs, but financed the museum building itself. We also thank the Federal Government of Germany for supporting the Bauhaus Archive during the first decades of its existence. Without the German Class Lottery Foundation Berlin, the museum would lack many a highlight. We thank the Museumspädagogischer Dienst Berlin, in particular Elisabeth Moortgat, for their friendly collaboration.

Annemarie Jaeggi

A museum for the Bauhaus
Introduction

The museum is situated on the edge of the Tiergarten park, not far from the Kulturforum and the government district. It was built during the second half of the nineteen-seventies according to plans by Walter Gropius. The aim of the institution is both to carry out research on probably the most important German art school of the twentieth century, and to adequately represent it: the Bauhaus, its origins, methods, results, and impact.

Eighty years after its foundation, the Bauhaus is not only a well known catchword, it has become something of a legend. It enjoys high appraisal, principally due to its reputation in the world of design. Rightly or not, the notion of a "Bauhaus style" has been created. International artists such as Vassily Kandinsky, Paul Klee, Lyonel Feininger, and Oskar Schlemmer took on a teaching obligation at the Bauhaus.

The educational reform concepts of the Bauhaus, developed particularly by Johannes Itten, Josef Albers, and László Moholy-Nagy, were soon adopted by international teaching programs in schools of art and design, and still continue to actively function there, albeit in a modified version. The architects who were active at the Bauhaus, in particular Walter Gropius and Ludwig Mies van der Rohe, belong to the Avant-garde of the twenties and are usually praised within the context of the International Modern Style (although they are sometimes criticized for faulty urban developments after the war). All in all, this little art school, which only functioned for fourteen years and had to change its location several times before finally being forced to close under political pressure, was astonishingly influential.

It would seem quite obvious to dedicate a museum to the Bauhaus; this, however, was far from the case in the nineteen fifties: after the closure of the Bauhaus and Nazi dictatorship, the emigration of many Bauhaus members and the war, it was no easy task to view, collect, and relocate the widespread Bauhaus legacy. The Bauhaus artists were not aiming at a museum context based on the preservation of their work. Had the Bauhaus not proven, despite expulsion from its land of origin, that it was an active idea worth following up? Indeed, former members of the Bauhaus still continued in their vocation, for the most part outside of Germany. Many of them, headed by Gropius, supported the endeavor to collect artwork and facts from the Bauhaus as a form of evidence of their success. They combined this idea with the wish to present the collection as a reservoir of ideas, an arsenal for future development. They agreed that the designation "Bauhaus Archive" was more appropriate than "Bauhaus Museum".

The Bauhaus Archive was founded in Darmstadt in 1960 by Hans Maria Wingler. The art historian and art critic had been doing research on the Bauhaus for years. This not only led to the basic documentation "The Bauhaus Weimar, Dessau, Berlin" (first published 1962 in German, 1969 in English), but also to a comprehensive collection of qualitative objects that called for a place of exhibition. The Ernst-Ludwig-Haus on the Mathildenhöhe in Darmstadt was such a place: for the first ten years, it offered adequate space to the young institution for activities and for its growing collection. Space, however, became increasingly restricted as time went by, and plans were developed for the construction of a new building. In 1963–64, Wingler convinced Gropius to submit plans for such a project, which, as it later turned out, could not be realized in Darmstadt. The association's support committee finally decided to accept an offer from the city of West Berlin to take on the Bauhaus Archive: the Bauhaus had been closed in Berlin in 1933, and now it was time for it to return to the city. An additional argument was that the Bauhaus towns of Weimar and Dessau were situated in the GDR and, for this reason, presented no alternative. Decisive for the move in 1971 was not only an improved financial situation, but also the promise given by the Senate that the building designed by Gropius for Darmstadt would be realized in a form adapted to the new site in Berlin.

Until this happened in 1976–78, the Bauhaus Archive was situated in the Schloßstraße in Charlottenburg. The provisional location already offered better working and exhibiting facilities than ever before. These were fully exploited; the collection grew, mainly owing to the support from West Berlin and the Federal Republic. Thematic exhibitions attracted attention to specific aspects and revealed new material; the Bauhaus Archive began building up a reputation in and outside of Germany.

The opening of the new museum building in 1979 with a comprehensive presentation of the collection was an event of international rank. Since works on paper cannot permanently be exposed to light, there was already a major conservational aspect which called for changing exhibitions. This practical fact supported the wish to illustrate the many facets of the Bauhaus in more specialized exhibitions, rather than show the collection in a permanent museum presentation. The opportunity to stage extensive specialized shows was substantially enhanced: they could be dedicated to the central figures of the Bauhaus, both in art and design, (i.e. Walter Gropius, Adolf Meyer, Hannes Meyer, Ludwig Mies van der Rohe, Vassily Kandinsky, Paul Klee, Herbert Bayer, Marcel Breuer, Georg Muche),

or else to other important artists of the period (i.e. Henry van de Velde or Walter Dexel). They could focus on specific areas of work (i.e. pottery, metal workshop, weaving workshop, typography and advertising, and photography at the Bauhaus), and also elucidate related projects such as Otto Bartning's anderes Bauhaus (other Bauhaus), the Hochschule für Handwerk und Baukunst (School for Crafts and Architecture) in Weimar, or the Hochschule für Gestaltung (Design School) in Ulm. The Bauhaus Archive is increasingly involved in revising Bauhaus myths and legends (what, for instance, is the Bauhaus style? How can the impact of the Bauhaus be defined during the Nazi period?). The museum also treats contemporary themes (i.e. architecture at Potsdamer Platz, or current teaching methods at schools of design). Still today the collection provides visitors with inspiration and orientation in creative design. To this end, a permanent presentation of a collection of objects rarely to be seen in public would be a further attraction. Limited space, however, means that many objects cannot even be stored in the building. Also, the museum shop could do with more room; the assortment of design articles, from Bauhaus to contemporary, is very well received by the public (and financially useful to the museum). An extension could be the solution to these problems and provide the museum with better facilities for topical events. Preliminary studies on such an extension carried out by Max Bill have shown that it could be realized on the site of the museum; its financing, however, is way up in the stars.

The Bauhaus stands for the great plan, still not realized on a general scale, to combine the artistic with the creative and the functional or (as expressed in the programmatic words of Walter Gropius in 1923) with art and technology. The museum demonstrates what happened to this program. At the same time, the Bauhaus Archive is open to current questions of design, as quoted in the subtitle Museum für Gestaltung (Museum of Design).

Looking back, Bauhaus has become more and more of a paradigm for an entire epoch and its desire for design; it stands at the center of manifold initiatives. Various institutions in Weimar and Dessau are likewise concerned with the theme Bauhaus. The Kunstsammlungen zu Weimar (Art collections in Weimar) have established their collection of art and objects as a Bauhaus Museum. The former Hochschule für Handwerk und Baukunst (School for Crafts and Architecture), also in Weimar, has been renamed Bauhaus University. The Thüringische Hauptstaatsarchiv (Central Thuringian State Archive) has comprehensive archival holdings on the theme of the Bauhaus. The Stiftung Bauhaus Dessau (Dessau Bauhaus Foundation), located in the former building of the Bauhaus, is oriented towards contextual research on the legacy of the Modern movement, with an integrated collection of art and objects. Moreover, a Bauhaus-Kolleg (Bauhaus lecture course) has been created. A plan exists to include the master houses in further Bauhaus-related projects. In the United States, the Busch Reisinger Museum of Harvard University Art Museums in Cambridge/Mass., and the Museum of Modern Art in New York, comprising the estate of Mies van der Rohe, both have an important collection of Bauhaus art and Bauhaus design.

Furthermore, the promotional term Bauhaus has been discovered by quite a number of people who are only marginally active in the actual field of the Bauhaus: there is talk of a Media-Bauhaus, or of Cyber-Bauhaus, of a restoration Bauhaus, of Bauhaus bedding, Bauhaus pullovers, Bauhaus carpets, Bauhaus restaurants, Bauhaus haircuts, and Bauhaus tights, even of a Bauhaus rock band. Last but not least, the European 'do it yourself' BAUHAUS store has succeeded in establishing the name for itself. Manufacturers of metalwork, furniture and textiles refer to Bauhaus series, and, unfortunately, the market is teeming with plagiarisms. This is evidently the commercial reverse of the coin for a global cultural success attached to the name: anyone wishing to bestow dignity and shine to a product refers to the Bauhaus.

Having been given the direct right by Walter Gropius to use the name Bauhaus, the Bauhaus Archive / Museum of Design cannot remain indifferent to these developments.   PH

The building

Not long after the commissioning of Mies van der Rohe for the building of the New National Gallery in Berlin in 1962, and inspired by the euphoria surrounding it, Hans Maria Wingler, founding director of the Bauhaus Archive, asked Walter Gropius to plan a museum building for the institution, whose creation he had been instrumental in influencing. Gropius couldn't say no, for many reasons. He had always insisted on the fact that a "Bauhaus Archive" necessarily had to be entirely independent. He could not imagine the archive as part of an existing institution, particularly not as a department of a larger museum, for it would lack the strength and vitality that were so important to him. He knew from his own experience with the historical Bauhaus; he knew that many decisions could only be made within an independent institution. In addition, ever since the Fagus factory, his first important commission in 1911, he was very conscious of a building's public identity. The Bauhaus Archive therefore needed its own high-profile building, comparable to that of the historical Bauhaus in Dessau. It had to be a monument which could compete with the politically inaccessible facilities in Dessau.

Provided by Wingler with a plan of a building site on the Rosenhöhe in Darmstadt, Gropius designed a complex presenting a slightly deferred H-formation adapted to the plot's slope. Gropius proposed to light the exhibition space through shed roofs. Wingler accepted the plan unconditionally, but was not politically able to implement the project. He had chosen the summit of the highest rise in Darmstadt for the building site. The city's officials deemed this too prominent a position for a newly-founded institute still in the process of de-

fining its profile. And then, compared to Mies van der Rohe's National Gallery, they failed to see the architectural qualities of the building. So, the comparison between the two buildings ended to Gropius' disadvantage when the Mayor made it clear that he would have accepted a design by Mies!

On one of his frequent visits to West Berlin, however, Gropius succeeded in awakening Building Senator Rolf Schwedler's interest in the Bauhaus Archive. He expressed the opinion right from the very start that the Bauhaus Archive should be situated in the city where the historical Bauhaus had carried on its last activities. In addition, he assessed the political context in Berlin as being more favorable to an institution of this kind than in Dessau. At the suggestion of the Senate, the Bauhaus Archive moved to West Berlin in 1971 with the guaranteed permission to realize the building planned by Gropius. Three alternative building plots were made available for the project: Gropius rejected the one situated in immediate proximity to the New National Gallery in order to avoid a visual confrontation between these two so distinct interpretations of New Architecture and not focus on the old antagonism. Instead, he chose the plot situated next to the Landwehrkanal which, in contrast to the strong slope in Darmstadt, was entirely flat. The necessary changes to the plan were carried out by his former colleague Alex Cvijanovic, in conjunction with the Berliner architect Hans Bandel. This process of adaptation turned out to be difficult and took considerable time. Drastic changes ensued as a result of political decisions and financial cutbacks. Wingler insisted on remaining as true as possible to the original plan by Gropius; this restricted the structural performance of the house regarding its adaptation to museum standards of the 1970's.

In 1976, the cornerstone was laid for a building that in general plan and silhouette was to be very close to the design of 1964. Important aspects, however, had radically changed. The great exhibition hall had been turned towards the South due to conditions decided upon by urban-planning, an extremely problematic decision in terms of museum practice. Also, the access ramp that traverses the entire building complex was added as a new element. The construction advanced rapidly and the keys were handed over to the institution in January 1979.

At the festive opening in December 1979, the collection, open to public view for the very first time, was positively reviewed by the press. The building, however, was seen in a skeptical light; Max Bill even spoke of it as a "screwed-up old man's design". Today, the ever-growing numbers of visitors to the museum evince a more favorable public opinion: the distinctive silhouette of the building has become a characteristic city sight, whereas the unpretentious inside of the museum evokes praise, as does the same feature in other buildings by Gropius. Apparently, the qualities of the building come more and more to light with advancing age. A sign for this tendency could be the building's registration in the list of classified monuments in 1997. In 1932, Berlin had given the historical Bauhaus a last abode in a disused telephone factory in the city's outskirts. Today, the Bauhaus Archive can present its collection to an international public in a representative exhibition building in the heart of the city. The good urban situation, combined with a well-founded collection and an attractive events program, are all factors which have contributed to the success of the Bauhaus Archive. The fall of the Berlin Wall in 1989 positions the museum in the center of the city, in close proximity to the government district and the museums of the Kulturforum. This, together with the opportunity of intense cooperation with the other historical Bauhaus sites in Weimar and Dessau, provides for new impulses. CW

1

1 **Walter Gropius and TAC**
Bauhaus Archive
Darmstadt
Model, view from
the Southeast
Planning stage
1965

2 **Walter Gropius and TAC**
Bauhaus Archive
Darmstadt
Perspective view
from the Northwest
Planning stage
1964

2

3

3 **Walter Gropius,
Alex Cvijanovic, and
Hans Bandel**
Bauhaus Archive
Berlin, 1976–78
View from the East
Photo Knud
Petersen, 1990

1907 The Deutscher Werkbund is founded by Hermann Muthesius. In the following years, the Werkbund already formulates central themes of what was later to become the Bauhaus. This is particularly the case in a discourse between Henry van de Velde, who underlines the importance of handcrafts in artistic creation, and Hermann Muthesius, who, in contrast, calls for higher standardization.

1915 Henry van de Velde asks Walter Gropius to consider taking on the post of director at the School of Arts and Crafts in Weimar. One year later, Gropius delivers a proposal to the Grand Ducal State Ministry of Saxony in Weimar concerning the founding of an educational establishment as an advisory center for industry, trade, and craftsmanship.

1918 The Arbeitsrat für Kunst is founded after the end of the war. Within this group, Walter Gropius, Otto Bartning, Adolf Behne, and Bruno Taut develop plans to restructure art schools. The project is a precursory declaration of the fundamental ideas of the Bauhaus.

1919 Walter Gropius is appointed director of the former Grand Ducal School of Fine Arts of Saxony in Weimar. The school is officially merged with the School of Arts and Crafts, which was closed in 1915 and renamed Staatliches Bauhaus Weimar (State Bauhaus Weimar). A manifesto and first program are published in April. Gropius calls for a reform in artistic process, rather than a new style. He postulates that art should be led back to its fundament and prerequisite in handcraft.

Since crafts rather than art are on the curriculum, the Bauhaus program is based on workshop courses.

The ideal of a labor community for all the arts corresponds to the concept of a unified work of art, the reunification of artistic disciplines – sculpture, painting, applied arts and crafts – to a new architecture.

Despite pursuing a utopian aim, Gropius' program is directed towards overall validity and commitment and towards the requirements of practical life. The plea is for artistic reform.

In the same year, Gropius nominates three artists as Bauhaus masters: the painter Lyonel Feininger, the sculptor Gerhard Marcks, and the painter and art teacher Johannes Itten. In addition, four professors from the former art school are enrolled.

At first, artistic tuition takes place in the teacher's classrooms, the craft courses in the workshops: in the first semester, these are the gold, silver, and copper forge, bookbinding, weaving, and graphic printing. In addition, individual courses on architecture are available; the architecture department itself wasn't opened until 1927.

1920 In October, Georg Muche is appointed master. During the course of the year, further workshops are installed: one for wood and stone sculpture, and one for decoration (later wall-painting). October also sees the start of a cabinet-making workshop; in May, a pottery workshop is set up at Dornburg/Saale. During this time, the curriculum at the Bauhaus corresponds to an apprenticeship, at the end of which an exam has to be passed at the chamber of crafts.

1 Walter Gropius, c. 1920

In order to achieve a closer relationship between arts and crafts, the workshops are headed, from the winter semester onwards, respectively by an artisan as "master craftsman" and by an artist as "master of form". Feininger takes on the printing workshop, Marcks the pottery; to start with, all other workshops are under the direction of Itten and Muche.

The "preliminary course" derives from a compulsory test semester given by Itten. This artistic preparatory tuition focuses on the basic properties of any creation: materials, how they can be formed and represented, and construction. The preliminary course serves the investigation of the personality and the creativity of each pupil, and is meant to establish equal pre-conditions of knowledge for the subsequent course. Until 1922, the style of Bauhaus products stands under the strong influence of Itten's exercises on rhythm, form, and contrast studies. Itten teaches the preliminary course, the backbone of the Bauhaus educational program, until the spring of 1923, with Muche taking on the summer months. The Bauhaus in Weimar experiences first public hostility. The attacks are ideological, but flare up in the context of artistic issues. The conflict is carried out during political meetings, in the press and in various publications, and finally in the Landtag of Thuringia. The state-financed school depends on the parliamentary allocation of subsidies; these conflicts, together with a changing political majority, endanger the existence of the Bauhaus.

1921 At the beginning of the year, Paul Klee and Oskar Schlemmer are appointed; in autumn, Lothar Schreyer takes on the new stage department. In March, a turnover takes place in the organization of the workshops: Gropius is responsible for cabinet-making, Schlemmer heads stone sculpture, Muche takes charge of weaving, Klee bookbinding. Gropius and Adolf Meyer build the Haus Sommerfeld in Berlin in an expressionist style. It is the first project involving the aspired unity of arts in architecture. The workshops for wood sculpture, wall-painting, glass painting, cabinet-making, weaving, and metal are involved in the realization of the decoration and the furnishings.

In summer, Itten travels to a Mazdaznan congress in Leipzig. Muche and Itten propagate this mystical doctrine of Eastern inspiration and are successful in gaining influence on a number of pupils, thereby adding to the inner conflicts of the school.

Theo van Doesburg, member of the Dutch artists' group "De Stijl", is in Weimar, with interruptions, from April 1921 until November 1922. Bauhaus pupils attend his lectures and courses, in which he criticizes the expressionist tendencies and crafts orientation of their school. He spreads his views on a new concept of constructivist design, favorable to technology. Although van Doesburg opposes the Bauhaus in Weimar, he influences the decisive turn of the school towards industrial design in 1922.

2 **Members of the Bauhaus and guests, Weimar c. 1922**

1922 At the beginning of the year, Gropius restructures his ideas about the aims of the Bauhaus. The major focus is directed towards reflecting on industrial methods of production and their consequences for design. In the summer, a conflict flares up with Itten, the central figure of the early Bauhaus, who rejects the new ideas and gradually retires into the background.

The first public exhibition of works by journeymen and apprentices is opened in April; July sees the presentation of an architecture exhibition by Gropius and Adolf Meyer. A Bauhaus housing-estate community is founded. Vassily Kandinsky is appointed to the wall-painting workshop.

During this period, the weaving and pottery workshops are predominant. They are the only ones able to make an appreciable contribution towards financing the school through the sale their works. From now on, workshop products of approved quality are branded with a stamp.

In September, Theo van Doesburg organizes the Dadaist and Constructivist Congress in Weimar. Among the participants are Kurt Schwitters, Hans Arp, Hans Richter, and the later Bauhaus master László Moholy-Nagy. During the same month, the première of Schlemmer's "Triadic Ballet" takes place in Stuttgart.

1923 In February, the Museum for Arts and Crafts in Zurich opens an exhibition with works by Itten and from the Bauhaus workshops. In March, Itten quits Weimar. He is replaced by the constructivist artist László Moholy-Nagy who heads the metal workshop and teaches the preliminary course from autumn onwards.

Following the departure of Schreyer, Oskar Schlemmer takes over the stage department.

First participation at the autumn fair in Leipzig with woven materials, ceramics, and works in metal. It is the first year of a noticeable workshop production, despite difficult working conditions due to the serious economic situation, particularly when inflation reaches its peak in September.

In February, preparations start for the "Bauhaus Exhibition", planned for August and September as a first comprehensive public account of the school's activities. The show presents products from the workshops and the classes, fine art by the masters, and an international architecture exhibition. The experimental house "Am Horn" in Weimar is the first independent building project of the school; the house is furnished by the workshops.

In August, the "Bauhaus Week" takes place with stage events, concerts, and lectures. The exhibition attracts attention to the school throughout the entire Reich.

Gropius coins his new concept in the slogan "Art and technology – a new unity" and thereby recognizes industry as a decisive power of the times. The concern with industry and mechanized production is determinant for all further work at the Bauhaus, and defines it to this day.

Since the winter semester, the preliminary course includes, in the first semester, texture studies with Josef Albers, in the second semester, the "material and space" course with Moholy-Nagy, the analysis and design class "color" with Kandinsky, and the design theory "form" with Klee.

1924 The elections for the Landtag of Thuringia result in a middle-class majority; the previous social democratic Bauhaus-supporting government is superseded. In September, as a "precaution", the new government revokes the contracts of the Bauhaus masters for April 1925. In November, only the minority of KPD (Communists), SPD (Socialists), and DDP (Democrats) in the budget committee vote in favor of the allocation of subsidies. The politically motivated and financially justified chicanery render a continuation impossible. Therefore, on December 26, the masters declare the dissolution of the school for April 1, 1925.
The "Circle of Friends of the Bauhaus" is founded in order to offer moral and practical support for the school. Marc Chagall, Albert Einstein, and Gerhart Hauptmann are members of the board.

1925 At the beginning of the year, negotiations take place with several cities concerning a possible continuation of the school, among which are Frankfurt am Main and Dessau. Some masters negotiate other activities. Certain former Bauhaus students, such as Wilhelm Wagenfeld, Otto Lindig, and Erich Dieckmann, take on teaching jobs at the institute following upon the Bauhaus in Weimar, the "Weimar State School for Architecture", under the leadership of Otto Bartning.
In March, the municipal council of Dessau, on the initiative of the Lord Mayor Fritz Hesse, decides to take over the Bauhaus as a municipal school. Classes start in Dessau at the beginning of April. With the exception of Marcks, all the masters of form follow the school to Dessau; many masters and pupils, however, are hesitant, and wait until the summer months to come to Dessau. Some former students take over the workshops as "young masters": Herbert Bayer heads the workshop for printing and advertising, Marcel Breuer the cabinet-making workshop. Then there are the workshops for metal, weaving, wall-painting, three-dimensional work, and the stage. Neither the pottery nor the wood and stone sculpture workshops are recreated in Dessau.
Gropius proclaims a new program dominated by the importance of industry and science for design. He declares that the aim of the Bauhaus is to achieve a "development of modern housing … from the simplest household appliance to the complete dwelling". Gropius calls for "systematic experimentation, both in theory and practice – in formal, technical, and economic fields". He describes the workshops as "laboratories" for the production of prototypes for industrial production. In June, the first "Bauhausbücher" (Bauhaus books) are published by Gropius, Moholy-Nagy, Klee, Kandinsky, and Mondrian.
In November, the Bauhaus Co. Ltd. is founded to commercialize the products.

1926 In October, the school is officially accredited by the government of the Land, and the masters are promoted to professors. Hence, the Bauhaus bears the subtitle "School of Design". The training course now corresponds to university studies and leads to a Bauhaus Diploma.
On December 4, over 1,000 guests attend the opening of the new school building in Dessau designed by Gropius and equipped by the Bauhaus workshops. The spectacular new buildings, the houses for the Bauhaus masters and the housing project in the Törten district of Dessau, achieve international fame. This propagation is supported by Gropius through publications and numerous lectures around Germany on issues of modern architecture and the Bauhaus. The buildings in Dessau still define the concept of Bauhaus architecture today.

4 The Bauhaus masters on the roof of the Bauhaus building in Dessau on inauguration day, 5 December 1926. From the left: Josef Albers, Hinnerk Scheper, Georg Muche, László Moholy-Nagy, Herbert Bayer, Joost Schmidt, Walter Gropius, Marcel Breuer, Vassily Kandinsky, Paul Klee, Lyonel Feininger, Gunta Stölzl, Oskar Schlemmer. Photo: Walter Gropius (with automatic release)

5 Students in front of the canteen, c. 1927. Photo: Irene Bayer

6 Weavers on the Bauhaus stairs, c. 1927. Photo: T. Lux Feininger

18

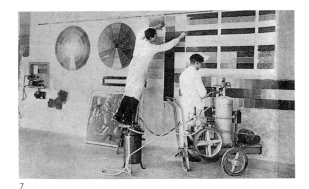

7

10

8

9

11

7 Workshop for
wall painting,
c. 1927

8 "Gropius build-
ing studio", 1928

9 Poster designers,
c. 1927

10 Weaving work-
shop, c. 1927/28

11 Metal work-
shop, c. 1928/29.
Photo: Marianne
Brandt

At the opening, the first issue of the magazine "bauhaus" is distributed; it appears quarterly until 1929, and then again in 1931.

1927 In April, a department for architecture is set up under the guidance of Hannes Meyer.
Klee and Kandinsky give courses in free painting; these are the first purely artistic courses to be available at the Bauhaus.
During the course of the year, the students become more and more politically involved. In July, Muche leaves the Bauhaus and is replaced at the head of the weaving workshop by Gunta Stölzl.

12 Members of the stage workshop on the roof of the Bauhaus building in Dessau, c. 1927

13 The weaving class, c. 1928. Photocollage from the portfolio "9 years Bauhaus", 1928 Photo: T. Lux Feininger

1928 Gropius resigns from the Bauhaus in April to go to Berlin to work as an architect. Moholy-Nagy, Bayer, and Breuer also quit the school.
At the suggestion of Gropius, Hannes Meyer is appointed director.
Meyer advocates a more scientific approach in the work and the classes. He considers creativity to be an objective process, which derives from rationally tangible perception. Meyer criticizes the former work at the Bauhaus, accusing it of being too formalist, and demands the exclusion of aesthetic criteria. This type of design is more socially founded ("popular requirements instead of luxury requirements") and is understood to be the most "correct for life".
The traveling exhibition "Young painters at the Bauhaus" is opened in Halle, before going on to Braunschweig, Erfurt, and Krefeld.
Bauhaus models are used for mass production by two light manufacturers. This happens later as well with weaving designs; until then, all products had been produced exclusively within the Bauhaus workshops.
The Bauhaus now counts 166 students; the Circle of Friends has 460 members.

1929 In April and May, the Museum of Arts and Crafts in Basle shows the "bauhaus itinerant show", later to be presented in Breslau, Mannheim, and Zurich. The exhibition shows a representative overview of the work at the Bauhaus under the direction of Hannes Meyer.
In May, the Federal School of Trade Unions celebrates the raising of its roof. All the workshops are involved in this building project, which remains the most important one under the Meyer era. In July, the workshops for metal, cabinet-making, and wall-painting are merged to a finishing department under the organization of Alfred Arndt. This is intended to strengthen the idea of subordinating all the workshops to the department of architecture.
The Bauhaus stage with Oskar Schlemmer's Bau-

14 Hannes Meyer, c. 1929/30

15 Ludwig Mies van der Rohe, 1932

haus dances tours Germany and Switzerland. Schlemmer leaves Dessau in November, leading to the official dissolution of the stage department.

A department for photography is created under Peterhans; the architect and city planer Ludwig Hilberseimer is appointed to the building department.

1930 At the beginning of the year, Bauhaus wallpaper is put on the market and becomes the most successful commercial product of the school. Student political involvement increases; accused of communist tendencies, the director, Hannes Meyer, is dismissed by the city of Dessau. Following a recommendation by Gropius, the architect Ludwig Mies van der Rohe is appointed director in April; he assumes his post in autumn.

Mies van der Rohe reorganizes the curriculum into five sections: building, interior design, weaving, photography, and fine arts. The program has a closer-knit timetable, and is reduced to five semesters. The architecture course becomes more important and strongly oriented towards aesthetic issues. The role of the workshops, and therefore of industrial design, is reduced. Mies van der Rohe underlines an apolitical direction of the school in order to keep it out of public political discussion. He even adopts disciplinary measures, not allowing students in favor of Hannes Meyer to enroll.

In spring, Gropius, Bayer, Breuer, and Moholy-Nagy design the German section for the Parisian show of the "Société des artistes décorateurs français". The show is internationally received as a great success for the Bauhaus.

1931 In April, Klee leaves the Bauhaus for an appointment to the Academy in Düsseldorf, Gunta Stölzl quits in October.

In November, the elections for the municipal council of Dessau take place; the NSDAP is the strongest party. The first point of their election campaign concerns cutting financial support to the Bauhaus and the demolition of its buildings.

1932 The interior architect Lilly Reich is appointed head of the finishing department.

Political debates at the school increase.

On August 22, a bill put forward by the NSDAP at the municipal council to close the Bauhaus on October 1 is passed with a majority of 20 to 5 votes from the KPD and from Lord Mayor Hesse. The

ky and Hilberseimer are requested to relinquish their position to staff "standing on the soil of National Socialist ideology" and the new curriculum should satisfy the "demands of the new state for its internal structure".

As a result, on July 20, the final dissolution of the Bauhaus is decided upon at a staff conference.

15 Raid on the Berlin Bauhaus. At the order of the public prosecutor's office in Dessau, the premises of the Bauhaus, which some time before had moved from Dessau to Berlin-Steglitz, were searched for illegal printed matter and other prohibited materials. From: Völkischer Beobachter, 13 April 1933

Razzia beim Bauhaus Berlin

Auf Veranlassung der Staatsanwaltschaft Dessau fand gestern auf dem Grundstück des vor einiger Zeit aus Dessau nach Berlin verlegten Bauhauses in Steglitz eine Durchsuchung nach illegalen Druckschriften und anderem verbotenen Material statt.

15

members of the SPD, whose political support so far had been decisive, abstain from voting.

Mies van der Rohe decides to continue the school as a private institute in Berlin. This is enabled by the income from license royalties. In October, a disused telephone factory is leased and provisionally adapted to the requirements of the school. In the winter semester, the school counts 14 students. Kandinsky, Albers, Hilberseimer, Reich, and Peterhans are still on the teaching staff.

On April 11, at the start of the summer semester, the Bauhaus building undergoes a police search and is placed under seal. 32 students are temporarily arrested. Negotiations with the secret police and other administrative departments close to the NSDAP concerning the re-opening of the school remain unsuccessful. The delivery of a new teaching license is made dependent of two points; Kandins-

The most prominent Bauhaus teachers emigrate over the course of the following years, amongst them Josef Albers (1933/USA), Vassily Kandinsky (1933/France), Paul Klee (1933/Switzerland), Walter Gropius (1934/Great Britain, 1937/USA), László Moholy-Nagy (1934/Netherlands, 1935/Great Britain, 1937/USA), Ludwig Mies van der Rohe (1937/USA), Herbert Bayer (1938/USA), Walter Peterhans (1938/USA).

1937 In Chicago, László Moholy-Nagy founds the "New Bauhaus", which already has to close the following year. In 1939, he then opens the "School of Design", renamed "Institute of Design" in 1944.

1938 The exhibition "Bauhaus 1919–1928" in the Museum of Modern Art in New York, organized by Walter and Ise Gropius and Herbert Bayer, shows the work of the Bauhaus under the directorship of Walter Gropius. The show leads to a wide popularization of the Bauhaus in the United States. Also in 1938, Mies van der Rohe is appointed to the Armor Institute – today IIT (International Institute of Technology) – in Chicago.

1952 Initiated by Otl Aicher and Inge Aicher Scholl, the Hochschule für Gestaltung (Design School) in Ulm is founded. During the initial years, under the rectorial direction of Max Bill, the school runs as a continuation of the Bauhaus. Former Bauhaus teachers such as Josef Albers and Walter Peterhans give guest courses.

1960 On May 5, the Bauhaus Archive e.V. (association) is founded in Darmstadt. Hans Maria Wingler becomes its director in the presence of Walter Gropius and other Bauhaus teachers. In August, office space is found in the Ernst-Ludwig-Haus; the official opening takes place in April 1961.

1962 Hans Maria Wingler publishes "Bauhaus 1919–1933", a standard work to this day.

1964 Walter Gropius designs a museum building for the Bauhaus Archive. The Rosenhöhe in Darmstadt is the designated building plot; the project, however, never becomes resolved there.

1968 The exhibition "50 years Bauhaus" is opened in Stuttgart, the largest ever Bauhaus exhibition until then. Realized essentially by the Bauhaus Archive, the show was subsequently presented in London, Paris, Chicago, Tokyo, and elsewhere.

1971 The Bauhaus Archive moves to West Berlin, where a realization of the Gropius design for the museum building is planned.

1976 Following the hesitant recognition of the Bauhaus by the official cultural policy of the GDR, Dessau witnesses the opening of the "Scientific and cultural center Bauhaus Dessau", where a historical Bauhaus collection is to be housed.

1976–79 The museum for the Bauhaus Archive is built in West Berlin. The original plans by Walter Gropius for Darmstadt are adapted to the plot next to the Landwehrkanal by Alex Cvijanovic and Hans Bandel. The building is inaugurated in 1979.

1986 The former Bauhaus building in Dessau is opened as the "Bauhaus Dessau. Center for Design".

1988 The Bauhaus Archive in West Berlin organizes the exhibition "Experiment Bauhaus" for the Bauhaus in Dessau. This first and only large exhibition in the context of German-German cultural exchange between the Federal Republic and the GDR awakens great interest within the GDR as well as on an international level.

1994 The "Dessau Bauhaus Foundation" is created in Dessau. It comprises the following departments: academy, workshop, and museum.

1995 A "Bauhaus Museum" is installed on the Theaterplatz in Weimar as a department of the "Kunstsammlungen zu Weimar" (Weimar art collections). The collection is centered on works from the Weimar period of the Bauhaus, until 1925.

1997 The museum building in Berlin is listed as a classified monument.

Prehistory of the Bauhaus

"From Morris to the Bauhaus" is a book title which has long become a slogan, positioning the Bauhaus in a line of development reaching back to the mid-nineteenth century in England. The artist William Morris (1834–1896) was founder and head of a reform movement whose aim it was to fight the damage incurred on culture by industrialization. From 1861 onward, he resuscitated old handcraft techniques in order to produce high-quality goods such as fabrics, carpets, glass painting, furniture, and utility articles. In his own "Kelmscott Press", he published books, paving the way for the Jugendstil.

Morris produced a reform wave which was later to reach Germany, where industrialization only set in after the foundation of the Reich in 1871. Germany had also recognized that well-designed industrial products represented a considerable economic factor. The educational system in England was examined in order to reform the German schools for arts and crafts. An entire generation of painters understood applied arts to be the major assignment. The Dresdner Werkstätten (1898), whose machine furniture had been designed by Richard Riemerschmid, are the most well-known example for the establishment of workshops all over Germany. The year 1903 marks the foundation in Austria of the Wiener Werkstätte, their most important representatives being Josef Hoffmann and Koloman Moser. A special role was played by the Belgian Henry van de Velde, who had been in Germany since 1897, had founded the School of Arts and Crafts in Weimar in 1907 and who paved the way for the Bauhaus. This was even physically the direct precursor of the Bauhaus, which took up work in the older school building.

In 1907, artists and industrialists founded the Deutscher Werkbund in Munich, aimed at improving Germany's economy by "enhancing craft work". The young architect Walter Gropius soon became one of the leading figures in the Werkbund. In line with the ideas of his teacher, Peter Behrens, he considered industrial building to be the most important contemporary form of architecture. For the Fagus-Werk in Alfeld/Leine, which he built in 1911 together with his partner, Adolf Meyer, he realized a façade with storey-high steel windows, a motif which was to become an icon of industrial architecture. In 1914, he erected a model factory for the Werkbund exhibition, in search of an expressive and inspired language for building materials such as iron and glass – which in his eyes were timely, but without expression – combining glass stairwells with monumental building volumes of Egyptian inspiration.

In 1919, Gropius succeeded in enforcing his art school reform with the founding of the Bauhaus in Weimar. Not only had he transformed basic ideas of the Werkbund concerning art school reform into reality, he had also captured the spirit of change of a young generation willing to rebuild a bankrupt post-World War I Germany. The name Bauhaus seemed to fulfill these expectations, and the expressionist style of Lyonel Feininger's cathedral on the front of the Bauhaus manifesto, which invited participation in this adventure, came across as modern and future-oriented.

MD

1

1 **Henry van de Velde**
Book jacket design for "Renaissance in arts and crafts", 1901

2 **Henry van de Velde**
Art school building in Weimar, 1904–11

2

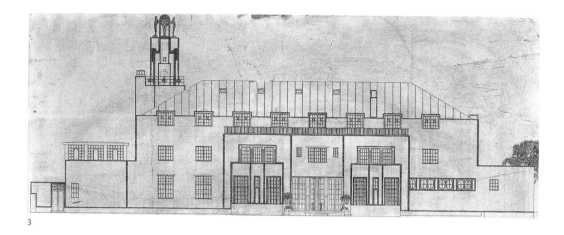

3

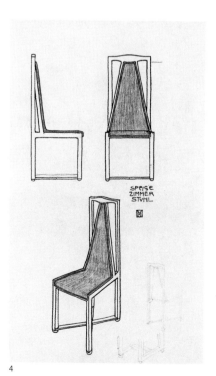

4

3 **Josef Hoffmann**
Design for the
Stoclet Palace in
Brussels, 1905
Copy with pencil
corrections

4 **Koloman Moser**
Sketches for a
dining room chair,
c. 1906
Pen and ink, color
pencils, pencil

5

6

5 **Walter Gropius and Adolf Meyer**
Main building of the Fagus-Werk in Alfeld an der Leine, 1911/12

6 **Walter Gropius and Adolf Meyer**
Model factory at the Cologne Werkbund exhibition, 1914

Das Endziel aller bildnerischen Tätigkeit ist der Bau! Ihn zu schmücken war einst die vornehmste Aufgabe der bildenden Künste, sie waren unablösliche Bestandteile der großen Baukunst. Heute stehen sie in selbstgenügsamer Eigenheit, aus der sie erst wieder erlöst werden können durch bewußtes Mit- und Ineinanderwirken aller Werkleute untereinander. Architekten, Maler und Bildhauer müssen die vielgliedrige Gestalt des Baues in seiner Gesamtheit und in seinen Teilen wieder kennen und begreifen lernen, dann werden sich von selbst ihre Werke wieder mit architektonischem Geiste füllen, den sie in der Salonkunst verloren.

Die alten Kunstschulen vermochten diese Einheit nicht zu erzeugen, wie sollten sie auch, da Kunst nicht lehrbar ist. Sie müssen wieder in der Werkstatt aufgehen. Diese nur zeichnende und malende Welt der Musterzeichner und Kunstgewerbler muß endlich wieder eine bauende werden. Wenn der junge Mensch, der Liebe zur bildnerischen Tätigkeit in sich verspürt, wieder wie einst seine Bahn damit beginnt, ein Handwerk zu erlernen, so bleibt der unproduktive „Künstler" künftig nicht mehr zu unvollkommener Kunstübung verdammt, denn seine Fertigkeit bleibt nun dem Handwerk erhalten, wo er Vortreffliches zu leisten vermag.

Architekten, Bildhauer, Maler, wir alle müssen zum Handwerk zurück! Denn es gibt keine „Kunst von Beruf". Es gibt keinen Wesensunterschied zwischen dem Künstler und dem Handwerker. Der Künstler ist eine Steigerung des Handwerkers. Gnade des Himmels läßt in seltenen Lichtmomenten, die jenseits seines Wollens stehen, unbewußt Kunst aus dem Werk seiner Hand erblühen, die Grundlage des Werkmäßigen aber ist unerläßlich für jeden Künstler. Dort ist der Urquell des schöpferischen Gestaltens.

Bilden wir also eine neue Zunft der Handwerker ohne die klassentrennende Anmaßung, die eine hochmütige Mauer zwischen Handwerkern und Künstlern errichten wollte! Wollen, erdenken, erschaffen wir gemeinsam den neuen Bau der Zukunft, der alles in einer Gestalt sein wird: Architektur und Plastik und Malerei, der aus Millionen Händen der Handwerker einst gen Himmel steigen wird als kristallenes Sinnbild eines neuen kommenden Glaubens.

WALTER GROPIUS.

Manifesto of the State
Bauhaus in Weimar
by Walter Gropius,
1919

Lyonel Feininger
Cover illustration
for the Bauhaus
Manifesto, 1919
Reproduction after
a woodcut

One of the basic ideas of Walter Gropius at the Bauhaus was that "the students should be inspired from two sides, from the artistic and from the craft side". He thought intuition to be as essential as rational analysis and solid handcraft, and rated the creative potential of Avant-garde art to be the basis for a lively, future-oriented work at his new school. This is why, although architecture had always been the goal of the training, at first almost only painters were appointed as Bauhaus masters: to start with, Feininger and Itten; then Muche, Schlemmer, Klee, Kandinsky and Moholy-Nagy. They guaranteed an outstanding artistic quality, a stylistic plurality, and an international flair, which was not to be found at any other school and has never been paralleled since.

Feininger's crystalline architectures and landscapes stood next to Schlemmer's statuary images of human figures, Klee's poetic world next to Kandinsky's abstractions. The primary predominance of expressionist tendencies was corrected at the latest in 1923, with the appointment of Moholy-Nagy. Coming from Constructivism, he was concerned with such elementary themes as plane and space, balance and movement.

However, pure painting class tuition existed neither in Weimar nor during the early Dessau period, since the Bauhaus was striving to detach itself from such academic structures. Instead of this, and parallel to their role as masters of form in the workshops, the artists were free to try out new paths in the tuition of artistic basics. Thus Itten, Muche, and Moholy-Nagy took over the preliminary course. On the other hand, Klee, Kandinsky, and Schlemmer developed individual themes and teaching methods, which were then partly published in the "Bauhaus books" series, such as Kandinsky's "Point and Line to Plane" or Klee's "Pedagogical Sketchbook".

The courses and the systematic pursuit of the laws of pictorial production were not to remain without consequence for the masters' own artistic work. Klee's pictures during the Bauhaus years reflect concerns from his teachings. Likewise, Kandinsky's painting shows a development from the earlier free language of form towards a more precise, geometric style, which most certainly lies connected with his teaching practice. In addition, the masters influenced each other and also absorbed impulses from the outside. The major exterior influence came with the Dutch artist, Theo van Doesburg, who stayed in Weimar in 1921 and introduced De Stijl aesthetics to the Bauhaus. Itten and Muche went in another direction: they moved from expressionist and cubist form towards symbolical figuration.

Of course, the painters at the Bauhaus not only impressed the students through their tuition, but equally through their works and their personalities. This was particularly the case for Feininger, who during the Dessau years occupied a unique position at the Bauhaus free of any teaching obligations. During this time, he was simply indispensable as a human and artistic authority, and held no regular classes. KW

1 **Johannes Itten**
Horizontal-vertical,
1917
Oil on canvas
Acquired through
the German Class
Lottery Foundation,
Berlin

1

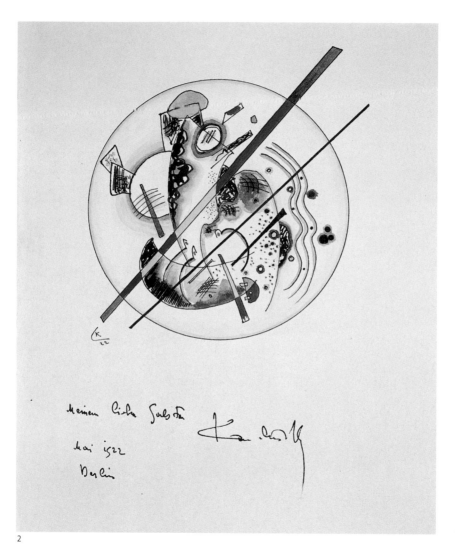

2 **Vassily Kandinsky**
Untitled, 1922
Watercolor and
Indian ink pen
From the guest
book of Gottfried
Galston

3

3 **László Moholy-Nagy**
Construction Z 1,
1922/23
Oil on canvas
From the estate
of Margarete
Leischner

4

4 **Georg Muche**
Two buckets, 1923
Oil on fiberboard
Gift of the artist

5 **Oskar Schlemmer**
Group with seated
person (Five figures
in space), 1928
Oil on canvas
Acquired through
the German Class
Lottery Foundation,
Berlin

5

6

6 **Lyonel Feininger**
Halle, am Trödel,
1929
Oil on canvas
Acquired through
the German Class
Lottery Foundation,
Berlin

7

7 **Paul Klee**
New in October,
1930
Oil, watercolors
and Indian ink on
cotton
Acquired through
the German Class
Lottery Foundation,
Berlin

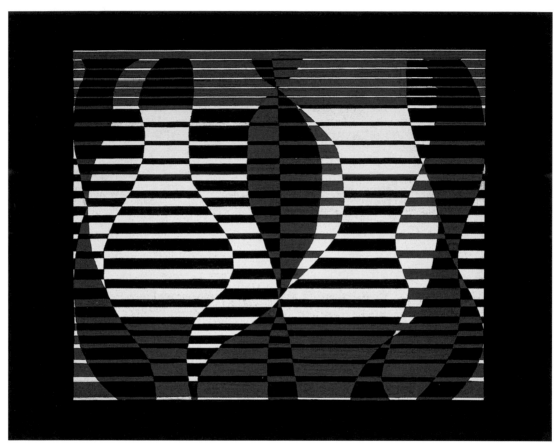

8 **Josef Albers**
In water, project for
a glass painting,
1931
Gouache

9 **Oskar Schlemmer**
Bauhaus staircase,
1932
Charcoal, graphite,
and color pencil on
tracing paper
Acquired through
the German Class
Lottery Foundation,
Berlin

Portfolio for Walter Gropius "1924 18/V"

The impulse for this unique joint work, presented to Walter Gropius by six Bauhaus masters for his forty-first birthday on 18 May 1924, came from László Moholy-Nagy. He defined the theme with a photograph from the newspaper depicting the announcement over public wireless receivers of the results of the vote for the Reichstag on May 4, 1924. The masters produced six variations on the theme, deploying in a most fascinating manner the entire spectrum of the artistic forms of expression at the Bauhaus.

Paul Klee's variant offers a clever diagram of a failed information transfer. A bright red arrow – symbolical of the message emerging from the megaphone – meets a fragile "ear" and engenders on the other side of it a little green exclamation mark. The message has been transmitted, even if only in a complementary color and therefore transformed into its opposite.

Oskar Schlemmer also reduces the newspaper photograph to a diagram. At the bottom of the sheet, a radio is depicted in a kind of technical drawing; at the top, one sees the anatomy of the inner ear. On the side, the ratio of the machine versus the human organ is expressed in an elementary equation: $1 \times 1 = 1$. The transmitter and the receiver are united in the action of communication.

László Moholy-Nagy transforms the motif into a purely constructivist composition, paying no heed to the meaningful content. Falling diagonals mark on three sides the instable frame. Receiver and sound projector become square and circle respectively. The leafless tree of the photograph appears as a black cross with its negative projection in form of a white inclined cross shape.

Kandinsky's dramatic composition shows a structure of litigating colors, forms, and forces. A yellow triangle – relic of the sound projector – strikes out from the oblique windowsill towards the center. The diagonal movement, many times interrupted by transversal barriers, is resumed through bundles of lines which finally lose themselves in the upper left corner in a system of calmly suspended circles.

Feininger transforms the image with soft irony into one of his characteristic marine scenes. He replaces the city dynamics with an idyllic moonlight coastal landscape. The windowsill has turned into water between towering cliffs, the street sign is now a moon crescent, the transmitter has mutated in to a little steamboat, and the sound projector is a huge cloud of steam.

Only Georg Muche hints at the confrontation of the apparatus with the listening crowd, thereby touching on the exploitation of the new wireless as mass-media for politics. Countless black and colored circles fill up the window opening and develop a disturbing energy which seems to surge forward and make everything else recoil from it.   KW

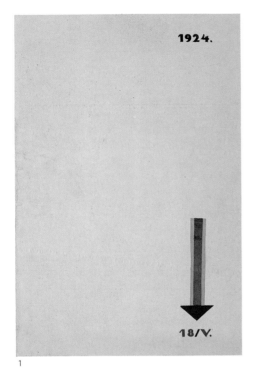

1

2

Portfolio of the Masters of the Bauhaus made for Walter Gropius on his birthday on 18 May 1924.
Acquired through the German Class Lottery Foundation, Berlin

1 **László Moholy-Nagy**
Portfolio "1924 18/V"
Collage and tempera

2 Photograph by
John Graudenz
from the
"Vossische Zeitung"
of 11 May 1924

41

3

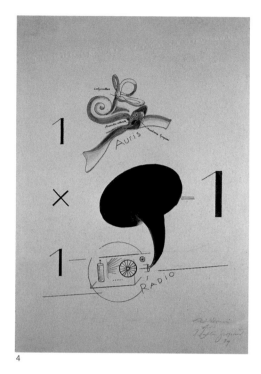

4

3 **Paul Klee**
Tempera on primed
cardboard

4 **Oskar Schlemmer**
Indian ink and
watercolor

5
László Moholy-Nagy
Pencil, Indian ink,
watercolor

5

6 **Vassily Kandinsky**
Indian ink, water-
color, and gouache

7 **Lyonel Feininger**
Indian ink and
watercolor

8 **Georg Muche**
Pencil, Indian ink
and watercolor

7

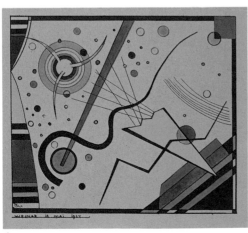

6

8

Johannes Itten's preliminary course 1919–1922

The preliminary course, as developed by Johannes Itten and continued by others after his departure, was part of the basic educational apparatus of the Bauhaus teachings. Preceding other courses, it was intended to teach students the basics of material characteristics, composition, and color. In contrast to his successor Albers, Itten's approach was neither purely rational nor was it directed towards a concrete result. He wished that the assignments be combined with sensual physical exercises intended to establish an emotional relationship towards artistic production.

His main point was the recognition and creation of contrasts which were elaborated in the most diverse forms and materials, whereby the reciprocal influence of two elements had to be accounted for. Perception, according to Itten, was dependent on the context. He considered that the contrast between light and dark was one of the most valuable and expressive means of creation. Studies in contrast were carried out on very different levels, such as in the field of natural materials and their textures, but also in the realm of free sculptural form.

A further focus was directed towards material studies, in which contrasting material characteristics had to be graphically represented and, at the same time, physically experienced in a three-dimensional construction. Through this, the student made the acquaintance of different working materials. The resulting studies should not be rated as independent works of art, but far more as exercises meant to sharpen perception and the expanded scope of creation.

The characteristics of abstract elements of form were tested in stripe studies. Itten saw the circle as signifying movement, the square tranquillity, and the triangle as indicating a strong contrast of direction. The characteristics could either be emphasized in drawing or else neutralized through the choice of a particular disposition.

Nature studies were meant to comprehend objects in terms of tone value and specific form, with the aim of reproducing them as precisely as possible in drawing, whether from nature or from memory. The studies were to be based on the inner experience of the object. These representations often define the material qualities of the models with astounding precision. Together with the investigation of contrast, form, and color, the "analysis of old masters" emphasized the emotional experience of form, color, and the dynamics of a work of art.

The favorite instrument was charcoal, which was fully exploited by the students for its general adaptability and great flexibility in shading. A variety of other works presented three-dimensional structures and collages. In the early years, the preliminary course was taught mainly by Itten, whilst Muche only occasionally offered an alternating program. Although the basic intentions remained after Itten's departure, a new structure was developed, distributing the introductory courses amongst other masters.

CW

1

1 **Friedl Dicker**
White and black cir-
cular forms, study
for light and dark
contrasts, 1919
Collage with white
paper and black
photographic card-
board, reworked
with charcoal and
crayon

2 **Anny Wottitz (?)**
Study in form, light
and dark contrast,
c. 1920
Charcoal, black
crayon, and zinc
white on paper

2

45

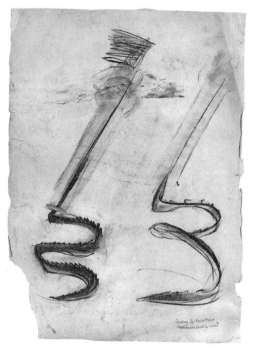

3

3 **Klaus Rudolf
Barthelmess**
Contrast study in
drawing after the
material study by
Mirkin, c. 1922
Charcoal on paper

4 **Moses Mirkin**
Contrast study in
various materials,
c. 1922
Saw-blade, leather,
and lamp cylinders
mounted on wood
Reconstruction
1967 by Alfred
Arndt

4

5

5 **Ima Breusing**
Orang-utan. Light
and dark animal
study, 1921/22
Charcoal, black cray-
on, and graphite on
tracing paper

6 **Franz Singer (?)**
Analysis of the old
master's painting
"Adoration of the
Magi" from an altar-
piece by Meister
Francke (1424).
Composition and
rhythm analysis,
1919/20
Charcoal and black
crayon on paper

6

Material studies with Josef Albers 1923–1933

Following the departure of Johannes Itten, Josef Albers ran part of the preliminary course and gave "material classes" parallel to Moholy-Nagy. Priority was given to working with materials, to the knowledge of manufacturing techniques on the basis of what would be needed in the workshops, and to the optimal usage of basic materials such as wood, metal, glass, stone, and fabrics. Albers aimed at conveying the essential characteristics of the materials and teaching his students how to deal with them. He thereby avoided anticipating workshop activities and excluded technical solutions. Only the simplest tools were allowed. This tuition also included "material drawing" as was practiced by other teachers: the board of masters believed that the class was necessary for insuring qualitative continuity later in the workshops.

When Moholy-Nagy left the school in 1928, Albers took on the whole of the preliminary course, further developing his material studies. Albers now made the students work with materials whose specific qualities had to be "discovered". They were made to handle the working materials without producing any waste: an economy of material and work in which both had central priority. During the first month, glass was the unique working material, after which one month of paper followed. In the third month, the students could work with an individual combination of two materials resulting from research into which ones were suited to one another; only in the fourth month was a free choice of basic materials allowed. According to Albers, the very particular choice of raw materials was meant to avoid recourse to solutions based on previous experience. The point was to develop an unprejudiced approach to the assignment and to work out any further working process on the basis of personal perception. The most important instrument of the course consisted in three-dimensional studies that had to be fabricated according to precise instructions and that excluded free experimentation.

In addition, graphic representation of the objects and their materials was just as much part of the course as the treatment of optical phenomena, most particularly optical illusions. Albers encouraged his students to work with photograms and carried out exercises in figurative drawing. From 1929 on, Albers' students could also practice precise freehand drawing.

The autonomy of the student, enabling both "discovery" and "invention", was a basic principle in Albers' educational program. In his courses, he tried to avoid practicing one particular working method. Instead, the student was supposed to "discover" and "invent" by himself. These preconditions led to classes with strong self-educational components. Albers' preliminary course, however, always followed a specific goal; there could be no mention of uninfluenced experimentation. In all apparent looseness of a particular assignment, the students were requested to work within certain restraints. The accuracy of the aim was meant to lead the student to recognize and develop his personal inclinations and aptitudes with regard to the rest of the course.   CW

1 **Eugen Batz**
Material study,
web of fabric, 1930
Charcoal, white
gouache on Bauhaus
wallpaper
Gift of Eugen Batz

2 **Pius Pahl**
Material study,
twine, steel cable,
tress of wool, 1930
Charcoal, pencil,
and color pencils
on paper
Gift of Pius Pahl

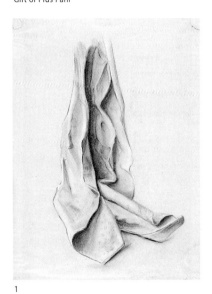

1

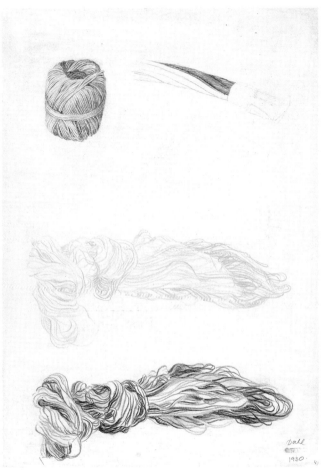

2

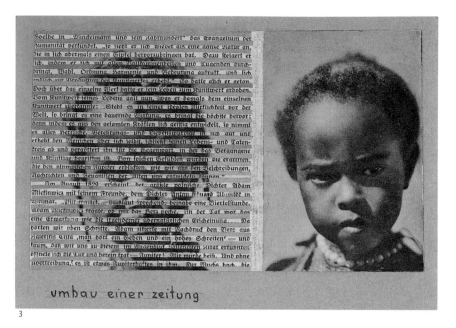

3

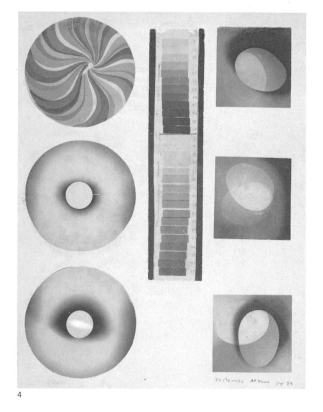

4

3 Hans Keßler
Typographical
study: modification
of a newspaper,
1931
Collage of news-
paper and
periodical cuttings

4 Heinrich Bormann
Spacial illusion studies
with blue print paper,
1931
Cyanotypes

50

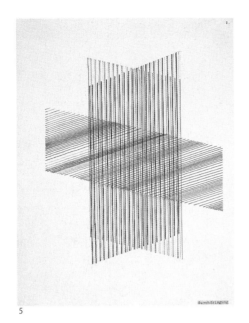

5

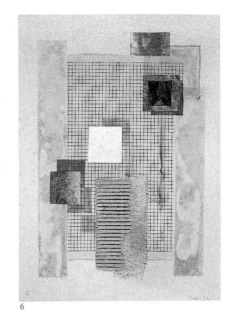

6

7

5 **Petra Kessinger-Petitpierre**
Interpenetration, spacial illusion study, 1929/30
Ink over pencil on drawing paper

6 **Alfredo Bortoluzzi**
Material study, c. 1927
Collage of different sorts of paper, corrugated cardboard, and fabric, partly watercolored
Gift of the artist

7 **Takehiko Mizutani**
Material study, c. 1928
Sheet brass

When Johannes Itten left the Bauhaus, the preliminary course was divided into two: Moholy-Nagy assumed the more theoretical aspects, and Josef Albers took over the practical perspective.

Moholy-Nagy's preliminary course was based on three major focuses. At first, the student was to learn to combine elements in such a manner that they corresponded to a preconceived idea. These thoughts were manifested on so-called tactile boards meant to educate tactile perception. The combination of materials on these boards was organized according to closely defined criteria, mostly laid out as scales in contrasting gradations of tactile values, for instance from smooth to rough in surface. In addition, values of perception, from sensitive feeling to basic recording, were to be fitted into a "tactile diagram" conceived as a general visualization of personal experience. The combination of materials enhanced their abstract qualities. These, in turn, were to be taken up in the drawings, whose ideal was a pictorial reproduction so close that it could be mistaken for the original. The exercises were meant to develop purely technical, rather than artistic "abilities".

The second focus was on exercises distinguishing composition from construction. Moholy-Nagy understood composition as being the creation of a balance between clearly defined parts through the modification of an overall composition by, for instance, the introduction of further elements. He saw this technique as a necessary preliminary artistic exercise. In contrast to this, the balance in the precise combination of forces of ideal constructions based on entirely preconceived technical and spiritual relations would be destroyed by the slightest change. The creation of a construction would therefore necessitate "a plus of knowledge" requiring conscious analysis.

The most well-known part of Moholy-Nagy's course was taken up by three-dimensional studies designed to sharpen the sense for volume and lead to the elaboration of constructive solutions. Here, studies in balance were of particular importance: simple elements and materials were used to construct objects in both visual and real balance. This condition was often quite precarious and the objects therefore exceedingly fragile. This is why most of them are known only as photographs. These exercises were designed to provide the students with the basics of visual aesthetics, such as measure and proportion, statics and dynamics. In addition, they were to be familiarized with qualities such as weight, elasticity, and density of the different materials. This regularly led to the creation of objects quite closely related to contemporary constructivist sculptures.

Despite Moholy-Nagy's systematization, his teachings were not uniquely based on rational thought. He himself repeatedly drew attention to the role of intuition in the creative process and underlined that it was indispensable to combine conscious analysis with the powers of dynamic intuition. Formulae alone could never be the unique basis for creation.   CW

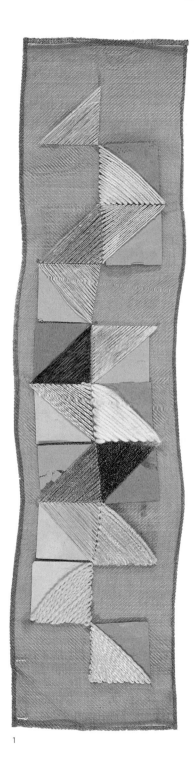

1

1 **Otti Berger**
Tactile chart, 1928
Various threads on
metallic gauze, on a
base of colored
paper sheets
Gift of George
Danforth

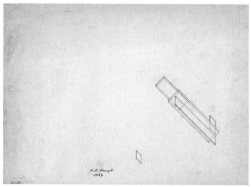

2 a

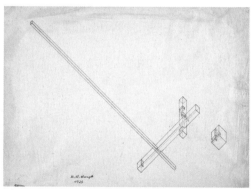

2 b

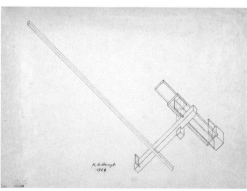

2 c

2a–c **Karl Hermann Haupt**
Three construction drawings for a balance study, 1924
Pencil on tracing paper

3

3 **Fritz Levedag**
Silver – red and
black, 1926
Collage of varie-
gated paper sheets
Gift of the artist

"Analytical drawing" and "primary artistic design" with Vassily Kandinsky 1923–1933

Parallel to the preliminary courses, Vassily Kandinsky offered classes in "analytical drawing" in which the construction principles of object arrangements created by the students from materials found in the classroom were analyzed. The students were to decide on primary and secondary tensions, to identify dominant elements, and to note down these points in simple linear drawings. These, derived from a sort of still-life structure, could substantially differ from student to student. There was no obligation for them to be unequivocal. The resulting schemes could then be completed in a free painterly composition.

The aim of the course was to understand the process of abstraction. Breuer's first tubular steel armchair can be taken as an example of such a study: the primary tension, carried by the frame, is realized in tubular steel, and the secondary tension of the seat and backrest is translated into textile belts, producing an optical contrast between both kinds of tension. These elements suffice for a functioning club armchair; the customary filled-in sides can be disposed of. Here, the focus on the awareness of the process of abstraction becomes very clear.

In the second semester, Kandinsky gave a course under the title "primary artistic design" which, in its fully developed form, presented the framework for a theory of design. It was built upon the basics of the organization of an image, the function of the center and the edges, and the characteristics of lines, planes, and bodies.

His color classes became particularly famous, especially for his association of the primary colors yellow, red, and blue with the basic geometrical forms triangle, square, and circle. Kandinsky explained the structure of different color systems, called attention to the psychological effects of color and dealt with the specificity of the non-colors, black and white. The studies, for the most part commentated and visually carefully presented, reveal both the systematic structure of the course and the range of possible interpretations of Kandinsky's teachings.

Kandinsky himself, however, was not dogmatic. He often relativized his own ideas concerning design theory, and remained open to other solutions. His professed relation between color and form constituted only one, and not even the most plausible feature of his tuition. He would certainly have been very surprised to see it develop into a highly popular Bauhaus trademark.

In 1928, Kandinsky started free painting classes in which he concentrated on the description in words of the basic elements of his art and the impartation of apparent rules thereof to the students.

CW

1

2

1 **Charlotte
Voepel-Neujahr**
Analytical drawing
with scheme,
1927/28
Color pencils on
tracing paper

2 **Charlotte
Voepel-Neujahr**
Color development
of an analytical
drawing, 1927/28
Tempera and pencil
on watercolor card

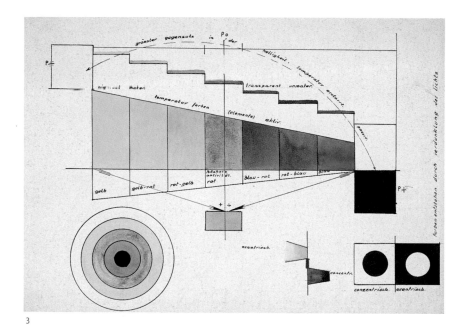

3

3 **Hans Georg Knoblauch**
Colors are created by obscuration of light, 1932
Indian ink and watercolor on drawing paper

4 **Otti Berger**
Inversion of the declination from white via the colors to black through a disposition in the dissonant diagonal, 1927
Watercolor on drawing paper, collaged on grey cardboard

4

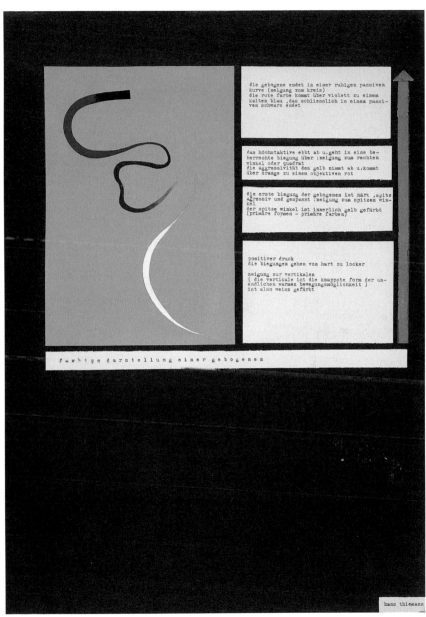

5 **Hans Thiemann**
Color representation
of a curvature,
1929/30
Collage with tempera
on paper and strips
of text mounted on
black card
Gift of the artist

5

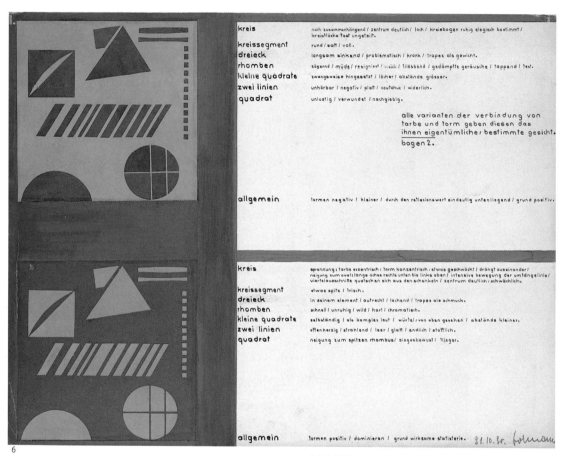

6

6 **Heinrich Bormann**
All variants of the
combinations of
color and form yield
this specific/ indivi-
dual image, 1930
Indian ink, tempera,
pencil and colored
paper sheets col-
laged on drawing
paper

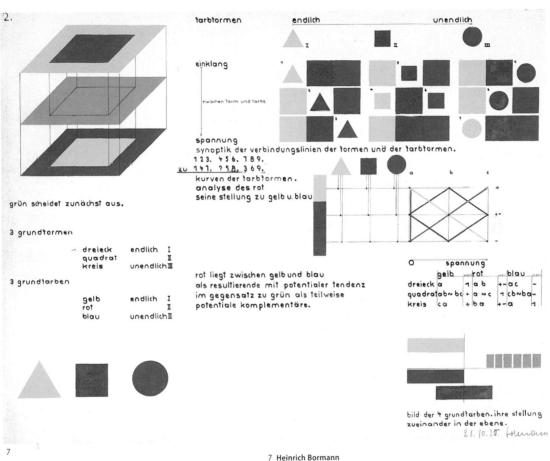

7 **Heinrich Bormann**
Relations between
basic forms and
basic colors includ-
ing green, 1930
Indian ink and tem-
pera on cardboard

Paul Klee's class was planned as a supplement to the preliminary course and as an investigation into formal means. His approach involved the derivation of everything from the characteristics of the line. Klee based his observations on the convergence point of two lines in order to discuss the third dimension and its perspective representation. It is from there that he developed the key image of balance in the form of scales. His expectations from a work of art were that it should present pictorial harmony, which he viewed as an equilibrium of movement and counter-movement. He illustrated the phenomenon of movement with the help of a circle and a pendulum, a spiral and an arrow.

Klee's color theory, based on a continuous principle of movement, stands out as an individual position in the history of such theories. Starting with the six colors of the rainbow, he renders this natural phenomenon in a related circle divided into six parts. The relationship between the colors in the circle results from two different kinds of movement: a circular movement around the edge and a straight one within the diameter of the circle, which he refers to as pendular movement. From the circular form, he derives a triangle of primary colors, which he subsequently expands into an "elemental star" including the non-colors black and white.

Klee's theory is a closed system determined by harmony. Although it seems quite plausible, it is in fact completely irrational. Only seldom can it be understood in logical steps; more often it appears to be purely associative and lacking in continuity. This made an understanding on the part of the students difficult. Nevertheless, the impact of his classes was large, most particularly in the weaving workshop, where he gave extra courses. Here, the focus was on the development of patterns through an accumulation of elements (displacement, mirror reflection and rotation, as well as interruption and inversion), a systematized division of planes, and the correlated creation of several central points. In addition, there were studies on the rhythmic disposition of elements of pattern and an extensive color theory. The square became a universally applied part of the exercise and can be found in many designs and woven materials which were produced. The choice of colors in many textiles is also derived from Klee's class. Postscripts from his courses attest to their dryness and strong practical orientation.

Starting in 1928, Klee held free painting classes available to selected students only. This art academy master class system was adopted by the Bauhaus for Klee's and Kandinsky's classes and the results can well be compared to those achieved in academic schools.   CW

1 – 4
Gertrud Arndt
Four pages with
elaborations from
Klee's class,
1923/24
Watercolor and
Indian ink over
pencil
Permanent loan

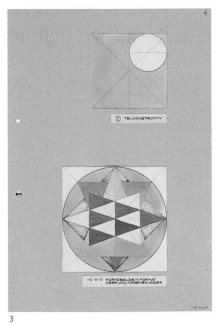

1

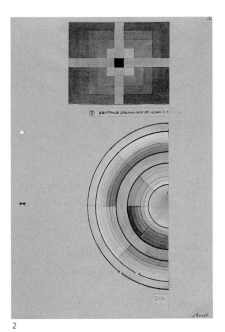

2

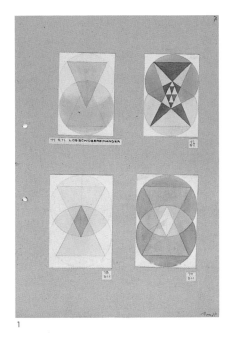

3

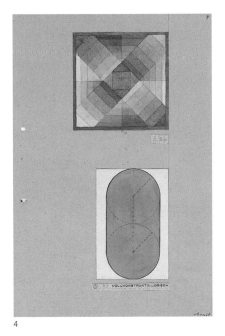

4

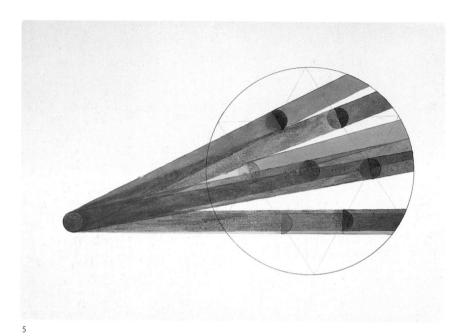

5

5 **Lena Meyer-Bergner**
Illumination/over-
shadowing, 1927
Watercolor, black ink
over pencil on
drawing paper

6 **Lena Meyer-Bergner**
Radiation/drifted
center, 1927
Watercolor, black ink
over pencil on
drawing paper

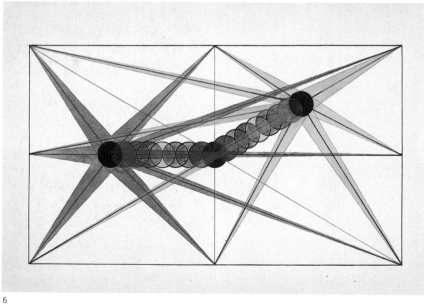

6

7 **Reingard Voigt**
Complementary
colors/direct media-
tion, 1929/30
Watercolor on board,
mounted on card-
board

8 **Reingard Voigt**
Economy of means:
combined comple-
mentaries positioned,
mirrored, and
reversed, 1929/30
Watercolor and
Indian ink on paper,
mounted on card-
board
Gift of
Waltraud Voigt

64

7

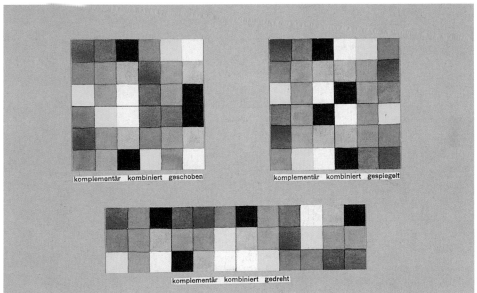

8

Life drawing and Oskar Schlemmer's class on "man"

Life drawing had always been part of the Bauhaus curriculum. Feininger, Itten, Klee, Schlemmer, and Kuhr held the course successively. Despite the rejection of academic principles, life drawing was esteemed as being indispensable. Since it was not, however, as highly valued as at art school, the results remained peripheral and, compared with the popularity of Itten's or Kandinsky's courses, were hardly noticed by the public.

Life drawing classes at the Bauhaus were organized according to non-academic rules. Different teachers set individual focuses. In expressive studies, Itten concentrated on the rhythmical coordination of the body limbs and on the body structure as a whole. Klee was interested in the representation of the tectonics of the human body through linear drawings, whereby the articulations necessary to movement were emphasized as dots. The studies from Schlemmer's class, far from being realistic representations, clearly show an idealized image of man.

In 1926/27, Oskar Schlemmer extended the life drawing classes to a course in general theory on the proportions of the human body, presenting a wide concept of man including formal, biological, as well as psychological and philosophical aspects. Here – according to Schlemmer's own words – we primarily dealt with "the schemes and systems of the linear, the plane, and the three-dimensional: the standard measures, proportion theories, Dürer's principles and the golden section. These can be applied to the laws of movement, the mechanics and kinetics of the body, in itself and in space, in natural and cultural (built) environments; naturally, there is a strong focus on the last theme: the relationship of man to his housing, to its appliances and furnishings, to objects." Schlemmer's theory of man was universalistic: he maintained that man, as a natural being hurrying through space and time, is determined by biological, mechanical, and kinetic laws. A part of the cosmological relationship between the material and the spiritual, he is able to create art and to reflect on aesthetic and ethical questions.

Schlemmer's tuition on "man" absorbs many influences. In contrast to other courses, the results found in the classroom had to be entered into prepared worksheets. The emphasis on conformity is a typical example of the attempt to scientifically rationalize tuition during the Meyer era.   CW

1

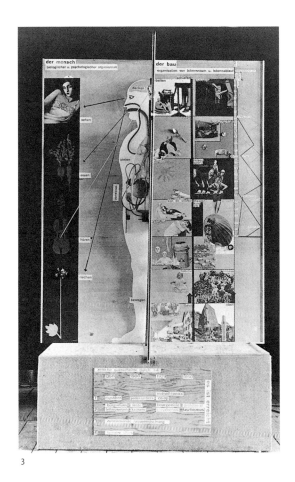

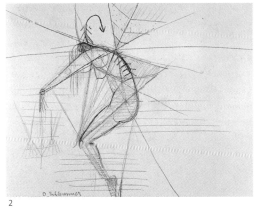

2

3

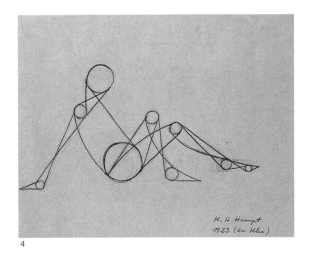

4

1 **Franz Singer**
Nude study from
Itten's class, 1920
Charcoal on paper

2 **Klaus Rudolf
Barthelmess**
Nude study from
Schlemmer's class,
c. 1920
Pencil on paper

3 **Man – biological
and psychological
organism**
Photograph of an
exhibition design
in Breslau, 1929

4 **Karl Hermann
Haupt**
Study of the body
from Klee's class,
1923
Pencil on paper

Paintings and drawings by the students

The Bauhaus was never an art school in the traditional sense of the term. "Art on its own is not teachable" can be read in the Manifest of 1919. The aim of the course was to produce a universal designer who would work creatively in architecture, handcrafts, or industry. Kandinsky thought that free artistic statement, particularly painting, could represent an "organizational support: ... the student will be led beyond the bounds of painting, but nevertheless aided by its inherent laws, towards a synthetic work of art".

Indeed initially, the majority of the students tried their hand at painting and drawing. And even in 1928, during the functionalist period in Dessau, it was surprisingly noted that the "Bauhaus had more painters than one may assume." Hannes Meyer, director of the school since 1928, reacted to this by introducing free painting classes, headed by Kandinsky and Klee. This, however, was a step which led to the isolation of art versus the other subjects based on rational and scientific methods. We know relatively little about the practice of these painting classes. The principle focus seemed to be the critical reflection of the artistic production of the students under the guidance of the master, in order to procure clarity as to the choice of the means and its relation to the desired statement. There was to be no tutelage, but far more the urge towards conscious and independent work. Such is a statement from Klee's painting class: "We had to explain what we wanted with our work, which were the means that we thought had led to the realization of the idea. Klee took a slate in his hand, drew with the pencil what should have happened in order to achieve the desired effect, discussed the

case with his small auditorium, rubbed it out and left the students to themselves to reach their own conclusions." (Helene Schmidt-Nonne)

It was in the nature of things that close contact to the big Bauhaus masters repeatedly became noticeable. In the early days, this occured with Franz Skala, who was clearly inspired by Itten, or during the Dessau years with the Kandinsky student, Werner Drewes. But the astounding stylistic plurality of their works was proof of the students' freedom to choose their individual artistic means of expression. They reach from De Stijl adaptations by Karl Peter Röhl to Surrealist tendencies by Hans Thiemann and Xanti Schawinsky, to early forms of Informel painting by Fritz Winter.   KW

1 **Franz Skala**
The dream, 1919
Oil on sack linen
Gift of the artist

2 **Max Peiffer
Watenphul**
Still-life with
bread, 1920
Oil on canvas
Gift of Grace
Pasqualucci

3 **Karl Peter Röhl**
Composition,
1922
Indian ink

1

2

3

4

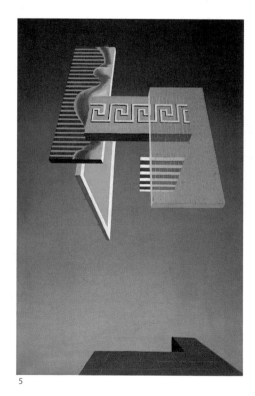

5

4 **Felix Klee**
Untitled, 1923
Watercolor, gouache,
and collage
Gift of of the artist

5 **Xanti Schawinsky**
Flowing architec-
ture, 1927
Oil and tempera on
canvas

70

6 **Fritz Winter**
Untitled,
c. 1929
Monotype

7 **Eugen Batz**
Yellow arrow,
1929/30
Oil on cardboard
Gift of of the artist

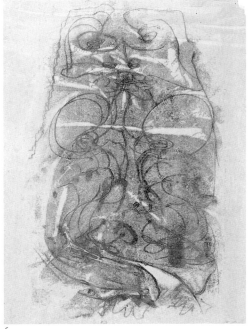

6

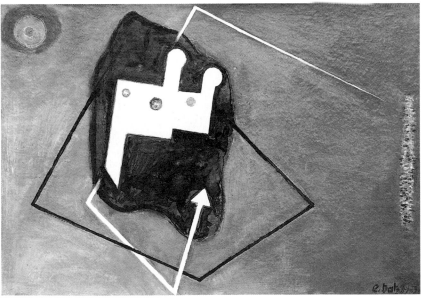

7

8

8 **Hans Thiemann**
Menagerie, 1931
Oil on canvas
From the estate
of the artist

9 **Fritz Tschaschnig**
Red door, 1932
Oil on canvas on
fiberboard
Gift of of the artist

10 **Werner Drewes**
Aggression, 1932
Oil on fiberboard
Gift of of the artist

9

10

Printmaking

A workshop for printmaking existed only at the Bauhaus in Weimar. In 1921, Lyonel Feininger was artistic director. Before that, the woodcutter Walter Klemm had been in charge of the workshop; Klemm had been head of the graphic class at the preceding Weimar Academy of Fine Art. Good technical equipment, such as hand presses to print woodcuts, etchings, and lithographs, also came from there. Master craftsman was the lithographer Carl Zaubitzer; he was supported by two journeymen for technical preparations and printing. The particularity of the art-printing department was that it did not train apprentices. In contrast to the other workshops, it was from the very start a productive workshop and provided the Bauhaus with supplementary income.

The production of graphic series and portfolios of the Bauhaus masters, started in 1921, stood at the peak of the workshop activity. The first ones, printed that year, were Feininger's "Twelve woodcuts" and Georg Muche's cycle of etchings, "Ypsilon". The Kandinsky portfolio "Small worlds" of 1922 was one of the artist's most important graphic series. The same year saw the production of a series of ten woodcuts by Gerhard Marcks illustrating the "Wielandslied", as well as Oskar Schlemmer's lithograph series "Game with heads". In 1923, a "Master Portfolio of the State Bauhaus" was published as the first title of the "Bauhaus Verlag" (Bauhaus edition).

In 1921, parallel to these works, the ambitious project of "Neue Europäische Graphik" ("New European Graphics") began: Five portfolios with which the Bauhaus aimed at bringing together not only the artistic forms of expression of the school, but in addition, all the important tendencies of the international Avant-garde – from Futurism to Dada, Constructivism, and Surrealism – were produced. The first portfolio introduced the Bauhaus masters; the consecutive ones presented works by German, Italian, and Russian artists. A portfolio with French prints remained incomplete. The names of the artists – from Chagall to Schwitters, de Chirico to Kokoschka, Archipenko to Severini – make clear the quality of this compendium of art prints from the twenties.

The printmaking workshop not only produced these series and many individual sheets for the Bauhaus masters, it was equally available to the students for their own works. Considering the large quantity of printed material still in existence, this opportunity was fully exploited. In addition, the printing workshop also accepted commissions from the outside, for instance for the printing of lithographs after works by Piet Mondrian and Alexander Rodchenko. Also, the foundations for the future development of "functional" typography at the Bauhaus were laid with poster and typography designs for various events and publications at the school. This included the Bauhaus postcards, which found wide distribution as original graphic miniatures and which, in their combination of typeface and image, were to become an important advertising medium for the Bauhaus. The basic change of focus, however, from artistic printmaking to commercial design and typography, took place in Dessau.   KW

1 **Johannes Itten**
Aphorism, 1921
Color lithograph
From the first
portfolio "New
European
Graphics"

2

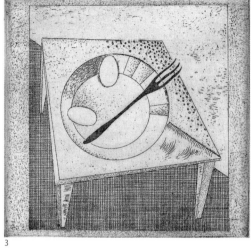

3

4

2 **Farkas Molnar**
Georg and El Muche
with the house
"am Horn", 1923
Drypoint

3 **Georg Muche**
On the table, 1923
Etching
From the "Master
Portfolio of the
State Bauhaus"

4 **Gerhard Marcks**
The owl, 1921
Woodcut
From the first
portfolio "New
European Graphics"

**5 Vassily
Kandinsky**
Violet, 1923
Color lithograph

5

6

6 **Lyonel Feininger**
Gelmeroda, 1923
Woodcut
From the "Master
Portfolio of the
State Bauhaus"

7 **Paul Klee**
Scene from
Hoffmann, 1921
Lithograph
From the first
portfolio
"New European
Graphics"

7

8

8 **Marcel Breuer**
Head, c. 1921
Woodcut

9 **Paul Citroen**
Lemon, 1922
Etching

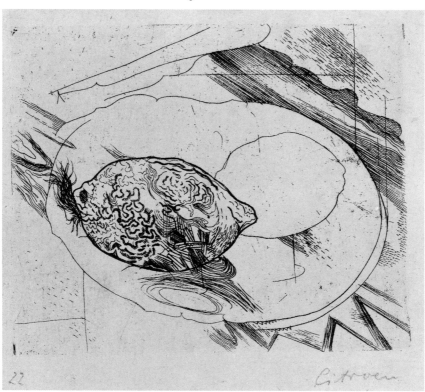

9

10 **Paul Klee**
The bright side
Postcard for the
Bauhaus exhibi-
tion in summer
1923
Color lithograph

10

Pottery

The pottery workshop was situated outside of Weimar, in Dornburg an der Saale. Starting in 1920, small groups of apprentices worked here together with the sculptor Gerhard Marcks as their artistic director and the master potter, Max Krehan. Krehan taught the basics in the crafts of turning, glazing, and firing in the production of simple utility receptacles, whose shapes and decoration remained entirely in the tradition of Thuringian farmhouse pottery. Then, Marcks enticed the advanced apprentices to try their hand at forming free receptacle shapes, which were intended to be sculptural rather than functional.

In 1922, the journeymen Otto Lindig and Theodor Bogler started to work on the development of new prototypes for utility ceramics which could be produced in small series by slip casting, but which were equally well suited to industrial production. These could be tea and coffee sets as well as straightforward vases and pots. With his teapots, Theodor Bogler devised a totally new principle: they could be mounted together from standardized basic elements, and according to a normed construction system, thereby presenting an array of different form variations. The aim, however, of cooperating with the ceramics industry was confined to trials. In those days, only very few manufacturers were prepared to experiment with the production of unusual pieces from the Bauhaus potters, amongst them, nevertheless, the Staatliche Porzellanmanufaktur Berlin and the Stoneware factories Velten-Vordamm.

When, in 1925, the Bauhaus in Weimar closed, no further pottery was installed in Dessau. The impulses from Dornburg continued, however, to influence the work of the ceramists who had learned their trade there. They set up their own workshops or found employment in the ceramics industry, and combined the components from their Dornburg period, the alliance of handcraft and serial design, for industry. In 1925, Theodor Bogler became head of the model department at the Stoneware factories Velten-Vordamm in Velten near Berlin. Werner Burri, also from the Bauhaus, succeeded him in 1928. Margarete Heymann-Marks was successfully producing her original serial ceramics in the Haël-Workshops in the nearby town of Marwitz from 1923 onwards. From 1929 until 1947, Otto Lindig headed the Dornburg Workshop and delivered designs to the Majolica factory in Karlsruhe. His crockery with unicolor glazes included models from the Bauhaus pottery, and was produced there right up until the nineteen-sixties.

Following the closure of the Bauhaus in Weimar, Gerhard Marcks and Marguerite Friedlaender-Wildenhain, his student from Dornburg, continued their work together at the Burg Giebichenstein school of arts and crafts in Halle. There, in 1929, an experimental workshop for utility porcelain was founded in cooperation with the Staatliche Porzellanmanufaktur Berlin. The workshop produced tea, coffee, and table sets, and also different vases in lucid, undecorated forms from designs by Marguerite Friedlaender-Wildenhain. Some of these pieces are still in production at the Berlin factory.   KW

1 **Marguerite Friedlaender-Wildenhain**
Jug with handle, 1922/23
High-fired earthenware, slip painting, salt-glaze

2 **Otto Lindig**
Cocoa pot, 1923
Stoneware, pale grey glaze

3 **Theodor Bogler**
Combination teapot with metal handle, 1923
Stoneware, grey-green glaze
Gift of Mirka Noesselt

1

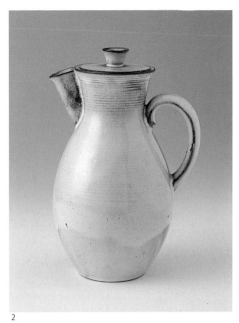

2

3

4 **Max Krehan**
(form)
Gerhard Marcks
(decor)
Bottle with handle and ploughing oxen motif, 1920/21
High-fired earthenware, salt-glaze

4

5

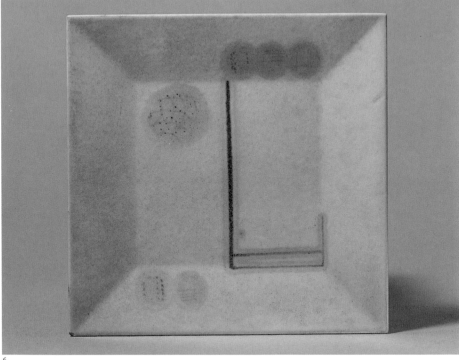

6

5 **Theodor Bogler**
(form)
Gerhard Marcks
(decoration)
Mug with portraits
of Otto Lindig and
Johannes Driesch,
1922
High-fired earth-
enware, slip paint-
ing, salt-glaze
Gift of Gerhard
Marcks

6 **Margarete
Heymann-Marks**
(design)
Haël-Workshops,
Marwitz
Square bowl with
geometrical decora-
tion, c. 1930
Stoneware, yellow-
grey glaze
Gift of of the artist

7

7 **Marguerite
Friedlaender-
Wildenhain**
(design),
Staatliche
Porzellanmanufak-
tur Berlin
Four vases
"Hallesche Form",
1931
Porcelain

Bookbinding

The private workshop of the bookbinder Otto Dorfner, a student of Henry van de Velde, was only affil-
iated with the Bauhaus in Weimar until 1922. The
workshop was at first under the artistic direction of
Paul Klee and was then taken over by Lothar
Schreyer. Later on, Dorfner continued to work for
the school on an independent basis. All the portfolios for the graphic editions of the Bauhaus were
produced in his workshop, whereby the cover
jackets were designed by Feininger, Klee, Hirschfeld-Mack, and others.

For a short period of time in September 1922,
a small bookbinding workshop was once again installed at the Bauhaus. Anny Wottitz, a student of
Itten, worked there independently. Her book covers
are often stringently striped in different qualities
of wood or leather; the titles are calligraphic or else
stamped with various type prints. Anny Wottitz not
only used conventional cover materials, but experimented with combinations of different kinds of
wood and twine, metallic foil and colored lacquered papers. She applied painting, marquetry, and
plaster reliefs to the book covers. With wholly
unconventional materials such as glass beads, fragments of shells, and elements from plants, she
finally left the realm of conventional bookbinding.
Her books sometimes have a near fetishist charac-
ter, thus the volume "African fairy tales" covered in
painted tree bark and plant fibers meant to pre-
pare the reader for the content of the book and is
reminiscent of the material studies in Itten's preliminary course. Her specifically individual book
objects remain today – with some few exceptions
in Surrealism or Contemporary art – quite unique
within the history of bookbinding.   KW

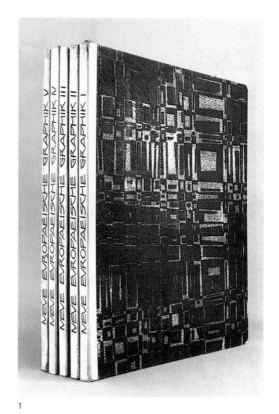

1

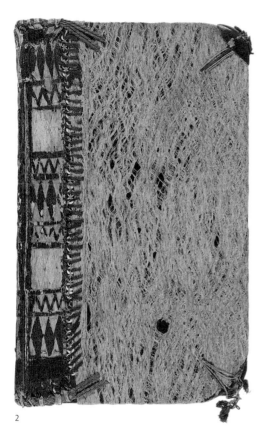

2

3

1 **Portfolios for the edition** "New European Graphic Art", 1921

2 **Anny Wottitz** Book jacket for "African fairy tales", 1922/23 Tree bark, elements from plants, glass beads, shells

3 **Anny Wottitz** Book jacket for "Chorus Mysticus", 1923 Mahogany and ebony, parchment, tempera

Sculpture

During the Weimar period, the Bauhaus sustained two separate sculpture workshops for stone and wood carving. At first, Johannes Itten was in charge of both in the role of master of form; Oskar Schlemmer succeeded him in 1922. The sculptor Josef Hartwig, who was to become famous principally for his purist Bauhaus chess set, was master craftsman. Well in accordance with the programmatic guidelines of the Bauhaus tending towards architecture, three-dimensional work for building was the main focus of the workshop. The wood carving workshop produced reliefs and wooden sculptures for the house designed by Walter Gropius and Adolf Meyer for the entrepreneur Adolf Sommerfeld in Berlin. The workshop for stone sculpture created wall decorations for both school buildings in the context of the large Bauhaus exhibition in Weimar in the summer of 1923.

Of the free sculpture created in both workshops parallel to these commissions, only little has survived. A good example for these works is the "Architectural Sculpture" by Otto Werner. Its massive structure, together with the complex spatial layering of cubic elements, are reminiscent of contemporary forms from "New Building", but evoke at the same time associations of a statuary human figure. The influence of Oskar Schlemmer is very clear; his sculptures and reliefs also present a blending of architectural and figurative elements, whereby the formal origins – as in "Abstract figure" – reach back to prototypes from antiquity.

Whereas in Weimar the emphasis of the workshop lay on free artistic work and the development of craft skills, Dessau concentrated more on educational aspects. The "Sculpture workshop", set up in 1925 by Joost Schmidt, offered in analogy to the classes of Klee and Kandinsky an elementary course in sculpture. The major concern here was the teaching of the basics of sculptural creation, "the awakening, development and intensifying of spatial conception, the conscious experience of spatial sensorial perception, and the realization of spatial ideas" (Heinz Loew). Practical fields of exercise were in stage design, the building of maquettes and the realization of exhibition architecture. With the consideration of movement within three-dimensional creation, some contiguity developed with the teachings and artistic work of László Moholy-Nagy.

KW

1 **Oskar Schlemmer.** Abstract Figure (Free Sculpture G), 1921/23, nickel-plated bronze, cast 1963

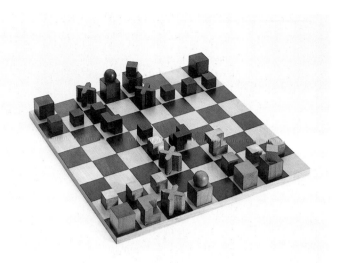

2

2 **Josef Hartwig**
Chess set, 1924
Cherry wood,
natural and black
coloration
Gift of Walter
Gropius

3 **Oskar Schlemmer**
(design)
Josef Hartwig
(realization)
Articulation doll,
1922
Turned and painted
wood

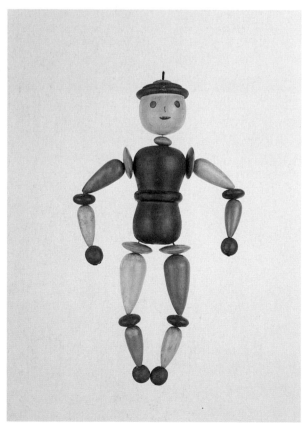

3

4 **Otto Werner,**
Architectural
Sculpture, 1922
Limestone from
Dorla
Acquired through
the German Class
Lottery Foundation,
Berlin

4

Textile workshop

From the very first, the weaving workshop was the domain of women. Already since Jugendstil, craft weaving rated as a profession particularly well-adapted to women; the connection between women and weaving, however, goes back to the nineteenth century.

Many of the women who came to the Bauhaus chose the weaving section purposefully for a later profession. In addition, the council of masters preferred sending women to the weaving workshop in order to "avoid unnecessary experiments" and be able to reserve the few other workshop places allegedly more suited to men. In the Weimar years of the Bauhaus, only particularly talented or persistent women made the grade to another workshop.

At the beginning, Helene Borner, the crafts director of the workshop, worked with all of the techniques of arts and crafts. Soon, however, the emphasis was concentrated on the technique offering the best conditions for a coupling with the Bauhaus program. Here, "experimental work" could be performed for industrial manufacture.

The range of products included cushions, tablecloths, piano covers, foot muffs, children's clothing, head-caps, blouse fabrics, children's bedding, but also sophisticated knotted carpets, Gobelins, and wall hangings. Sometimes weavers were employed to carry out the designs. The workshop in Weimar was equipped with a jacquard loom.

The female pupils learned the basic impulses for pattern and color design in the classes of Johannes Itten, Georg Muche, and later, Paul Klee. Although "function" in weaving was one of the magic words, for a long time a strong aesthetic orientation could still be felt. This stood in the way of the required functionality: contrasts between thick and thin or mat and glossy thread were often primarily of aesthetic relevance and posed more of a hindrance in usage than anything else.

In 1927, the workshop was taken over by Gunta Stölzl. Succeeding Gertrud Grunow, who had been master for harmonizing theory during the Weimar period, and Helene Börner, head of crafts, she was given the title of young master – with less rights, however, than her male colleagues.

Stölzl not only entirely re-equipped the workshop in Dessau, she also created an educational course over eight semesters, starting with an apprenticeship and ending with a journeyman's examination, re-rated after 1929 as a Diploma.

The workshop now experimented with synthetic fibers such as cellophane and also rayon, a new thread which at that time revolutionized the entire textile market. Robust steel yarn was developed for the use on tubular steel chairs.

After Stölzl's departure in 1931, Lilly Reich and Otti Berger set new accents. The two last years of the Bauhaus saw the production of three textile albums (in the dimensions of the wallpaper books). Due to the interruption of their product licensing in 1933, however, they never succeeded in reaching the popularity of the Bauhaus wallpaper. The simplicity and unassuming modesty of these textiles stand in strong contrast to the earlier fabrics.   MD

1 **Max Peiffer
Watenphul**
Wall hanging,
c. 1921
Gobelin, wool,
hemp
Gift of
Johannes Itten

1

2

3

2 **Gertrud Arndt**
Design for a knotted carpet in the director's office of Walter Gropius, 1923
Watercolor and pencil

3 **Gunta Stölzl**
Design for a half-gobelin, 1927/28
Gouache, Indian ink, pencil

4

4 **Ida Kerkovius**
Blanket, c. 1921
Applications on felt

5

5 **Anni Albers**
Wall hanging,
1926/1965
Cotton and rayon

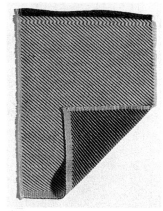

6

6a

7

6 **Otti Berger /
Lilly Reich**
Fabric sample from
a Bauhaus textile
album, 1932/33
Cotton and rayon

6a **Anni Albers**
Cellophane up-
holstery fabric for
the Trade Union
School in Bernau,
1928–30

7 **Ruth Hollos-
Consemüller**
Gobelin, c. 1930
Cotton and wool

96

8 **Gunta Stölzl**
Gobelin
"red-green",
1927/28
Cotton, wool, silk,
linen   8

Cabinet-making workshop

No workshop has marked the public image of the Bauhaus as much as the cabinet-making workshop. At first it was directed by Johannes Itten, then in 1921, Walter Gropius became master of form and had part of the furnishings for his buildings realized there.

The "experimental house am Horn", built for the Bauhaus exhibition of 1923, conveys one of the earliest and most radical visions of a "new living" style. At the same time, Gropius, in furnishing his director's office without obeying the dictate of traditional forms of representation, created a modern "Gesamtkunstwerk". For the first time, the exhibition presented furniture visibly built along the basic lines of Gropius' Bauhaus concept, according to which each object should fulfill its practical function, be long-lasting, cheap, good-looking, and also well-suited as a prototype for industrial production. Breuer's lattice chair seemed to fulfill Gropius' instructions to the letter: aesthetically pleasant and possessing an inherent analysis of function, this chair-sculpture became one of the most famous designs from the Bauhaus in Weimar.

In 1925 in Dessau, Breuer, now appointed head of the workshop, could realize his radical designs with the help of tubular steel. A series of chairs was created, exploiting the technical potentials of the new material, simplifying the idea of a traditional chair, and providing it with a completely new appearance, underlined by the light-reflecting steel surface. This furniture became the symbol of a new living style and the quintessence of the new orientation of the Bauhaus in Dessau. In many of the interior decoration projects carried out until 1930, Breuer combined his chairs with sparse and simple box furniture made of wood, often developed from a single module and fixed to the wall in a band.

When Breuer left in 1928, the aims of the workshop changed under new direction: the production of singular pieces with a design typical of the Bauhaus philosophy was replaced by a profile of furniture based on simple materials and made specifically for industrial production. Hannes Meyer invented the appropriate slogan "popular requirements instead of luxury requirements". Model furnishings proposed by the Bauhaus bear witness to the change; since the spectrum had been numerically reduced, many of the individual pieces had to be multi-functional. Their design intentionally avoided aesthetic richness and, underscored by the usage of specific materials, repressed any handcrafted effect.

When Mies van der Rohe became director, the workshop was basically closed down, commissions being rare due to the difficult economic situation. In addition, Mies considered the alliance between production enterprise and school to be contradictory. He had developed his famous tubular steel and steel strip furniture long before he became director of the Bauhaus. It is their model function which led them to become Bauhaus furniture: students were convinced that they needed these models in order to reach a compositional entity in their designs comparable to that achieved by Mies in his architecture. The last phase of the Bauhaus was marked by prototypes of inimitable aesthetic quality. The work of Mies' students would have been unthinkable without these products.   CW

1 **Walter Gropius**
Sideboard for
periodicals, 1923
Cherry wood, glass
plate

2 **Erich Dieckmann**
Dining-room chair,
1923
Cherry wood,
leather

3 **Erich Dieckmann**
Desk chair, 1923
Cherry wood,
leather

1

2

3

4 **Marcel Breuer**
Square table hti 9,
1924
Cherry wood

4

5 **Marcel Breuer**
Chair lti 2 and stool
rti 13, 1924
Stained oak, woven
horsehair

5

6 **Marcel Breuer**
Chair, ti 1a, 1924
Stained maple,
woven horsehair

6

7

7 **Marcel Breuer**
Children's chair
ti 3a, kitchen chair
ti 3d, 1923
Beech and
lacquered plywood

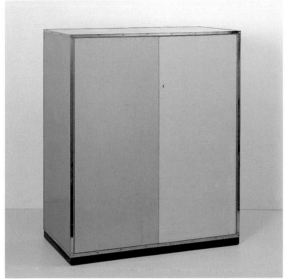

8

9

10

8 Marcel Breuer
Half-size wardrobe from the Vogler consultation room, 1929
Lacquered plywood on slats of pine, nickel-plated brass strips

9 Marcel Breuer
Large double-sided desk from the Vogler consultation room, 1929
Lacquered joinered tabletop, linoleum covering, nickel-plated brass strips

10 Marcel Breuer
Broom cupboard from Vogler's private apartment, 1929
Lacquered pine, nickel-plated steel bar

11 **Marcel Breuer**
Armchair B3,
1925/26
Nickel-plated
tubular steel,
iron thread fabric
11

12

12 **Marcel Breuer**
Chair B33, 1928
Produced by Thonet
Nickel-plated tubu-
lar steel, iron thread
fabric

13 **Marcel Breuer**
Table set B9 a–d,
1926
Produced by
Standard-Möbel
Nickel-plated tubu-
lar steel, lacquered
joinered tabletops

13

14

14 **Josef Pohl**
Wardrobe element
on wheels, 1929/30
Plywood on slat
frame

15 **Interior decora-
tion workshop**
Kredenz ti 270, 1930
Cherry wood, linole-
um, nickel-plated
brass strips

15

16

17

18

16 **Josef Albers**
Armchair, 1928
Walnut and maple
wood, upholstery

17 **Interior decora-
tion workshop
(Alfred Arndt ?)**
Chair, 1927/29
Stained beech, pine
seat, back- and arm-
rests

18 **Hin Bredendieck,
Hermann Gautel**
Work chair me
1002, 1930
Chrome-plated
tubular steel,
plywood

Metal workshop

In line with the overall guidelines of the early Bauhaus, the metal workshop in Weimar, which at first ran under the name of gold, silver, and copper forge, taught traditional metal working techniques. Johannes Itten was the artistic director during the first years, and then in 1922, the experienced silversmith Christian Dell took on the position of master craftsman until 1925. The student's production clearly stood under the influence of Itten's teachings: the main concern in the production of vessels and appliances was the free study of form together with the experimentally acquired knowledge of metallic materials and their possible treatment. Naum Slutzky's spherical copper tin is characteristic of these early works.

When, in 1923, László Moholy-Nagy became head of the workshop, the focus was directed towards more functional aspects. Straightforward vessels reduced to elementary forms in brass, nickel-plated brass or silver were produced. These, as with Marianne Brandt's silver set, or Gyula Pap's candleholder with seven arms, were indeed conceived for industrial serial production, but realized only as single pieces or in hand-crafted series. This was the period in which the first lamp models were produced, namely the legendary "Bauhaus lamp" by Carl Jakob Jucker and Wilhelm Wagenfeld: "a cheap, practical lighting device, beautiful through simplicity", as Josef Albers praised it, although even then the lamp was not cheap, due to its hand-crafted fabrication.

In Dessau, the more professional and extensive workshop's equipment was capable of accommodating a more rational serial production of vessels and appliances. Already in 1926, the metal workshop mastered the design and production of all the lighting requirements for the new Bauhaus building. In the following years, it became more and more a "design laboratory" for new lighting equipment and, finally, when several industrial lighting manufacturers took the models into serial production, it achieved the status of one of the most effective and successful workshops at the Bauhaus. The production of some of the types, such as the Kandem lamps by Marianne Brandt and Hin Bredendieck, was continued for many years after the closure of the Bauhaus.   KW

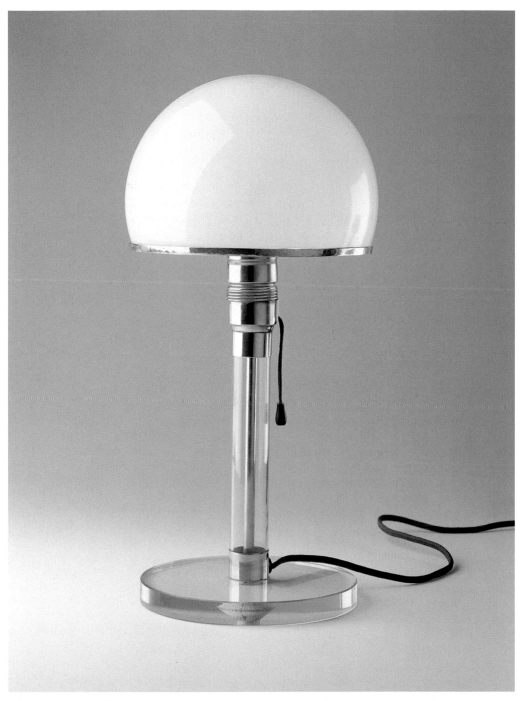

1 **Carl Jakob Jucker and Wilhelm Wagenfeld.** Table lamp, 1923/24, nickel-plated brass, glass, opaque glass, gift of Herbert Skrebba

2

3

2 **Gyula Pap**
Candleholder with
seven arms, 1922
Brass
Gift of Gerda
Niemann

3 **Naum Slutzky**
Spherical tin, 1920
Copper, pewter
interior
Gift of Gerda
Niemann

4 **Christian Dell**
Wine jug, 1922
New silver, ebony

5 **Josef Albers**
Fruit bowl, 1923
Chrome plated
brass, glass, black
lacquered wood
Gift of Josef Albers

4

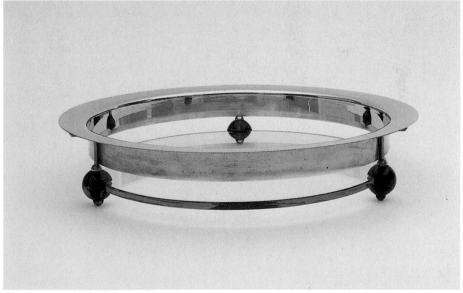

5

6 **Marianne Brandt**
Tea-extract pot,
1924
Brass, silver, ebony
Gift of Willy
Hauswald

7 **Marianne Brandt**
Tea and coffee set,
1924
Silver, ebony, glass
Acquired through
the German Class
Lottery Foundation,
Berlin

6

7

8 **Marianne Brandt
and Hin Bredendieck**
(design)
Körting&Mathiesen,
Leipzig (realization)
Kandem desk-lamp,
1928
Bronze and steel
plate
Gift of Fritz Körting

9

9 **Marianne Brandt
and Helmut Schulze**
(design)
Körting&Mathiesen,
Leipzig (realization)
Kandem double
cylinder lamp, 1928
Nickel-plated brass,
opaque glass

8

113

Typography and commercial art

In the first years of the Bauhaus at Weimar, typography, the style and arrangement of characters, did not yet play the central role it was later to take on. For Johannes Itten and Lothar Schreyer, calligraphy was essentially an artistic means of expression. Itten, together with his students, experimented with the visual expression of literary content via expressionist forms of lettering, or with the combination of various type prints and letter sizes. In his course on the form of writing, Lothar Schreyer studied calligraphic exercises and designed alphabets on the basis of geometrical systems of construction. At first, practical fields of application remained seldom and were restricted to school invitations and miscellaneous printed matters.

With the appointment of Moholy-Nagy in 1923, who was to introduce the ideas of "New Typography" to the Bauhaus, the situation radically changed. He considered typescript to be primarily a communications medium, and was concerned with the "clarity of the message in its most emphatic form". His influence is already clearly visible in 1923 in the publicity campaign for the large Bauhaus exhibition of summer 1923. Moholy-Nagy designed the layout for the exhibition publication and further took over the typography of the "Bauhaus books". Fourteen volumes, of which the first appeared in 1925, were to be published. From then on, typography at the Bauhaus was closely connected to corporate identity and to the development of an unmistakable image for the school. Characteristic for the design were clear, unadorned type prints, the articulation and accentuation of pages through distinct symbols or typographic elements highlighted in color, and finally direct information in a combination of text and photography, for which the name "Typofoto" was found. In addition, the consideration of economic factors led to the usage of normed formats, a partly simplified spelling, and more particularly, the abolition of capitalization. In Weimar, next to Moholy-Nagy, both Joost Schmidt and Herbert Bayer had also been concerned with typography. In Dessau, Bayer took over the newly installed workshop for printing and advertising and rapidly transformed it into a professionally functioning studio for graphic design, supported more and more by commissions from the outside. He intensively developed Avant-garde typesetting with the "Universal" or "Bayertype", and his posters and printed matters show a concern with modern themes from the psychology of advertising. Following his departure from the Bauhaus in 1928, Bayer continued to work at first in Germany, later in the USA, and became one of the most influential graphic designers of the twentieth century.

Joost Schmidt was his successor at the Bauhaus. He introduced a systematic course for the design of lettering and advertising graphics and expanded it to the practice of exhibition design. Examples of the applicability of experimental forms of presentation in architecture, sculpture, photography, and typography were presented in Bauhaus traveling exhibitions and at conventions in and outside Germany. The stands were designed by the advertising workshop.   KW

1

1 **Lothar Schreyer**
Letter picture
"Sanctifica me",
1923
Color lithograph

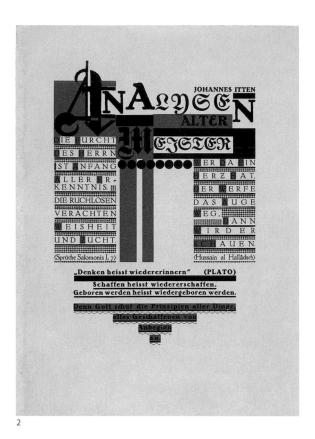

2

2 **Johannes Itten**
Page from the
"Analysis of old
masters" in "Utopia.
Dokumente der
Wirklichkeit", 1921
Lithograph

3
László Moholy-Nagy
Title page of
"Staatliches
Bauhaus in Weimar
1919–1923", 1923
Letterpress print

3

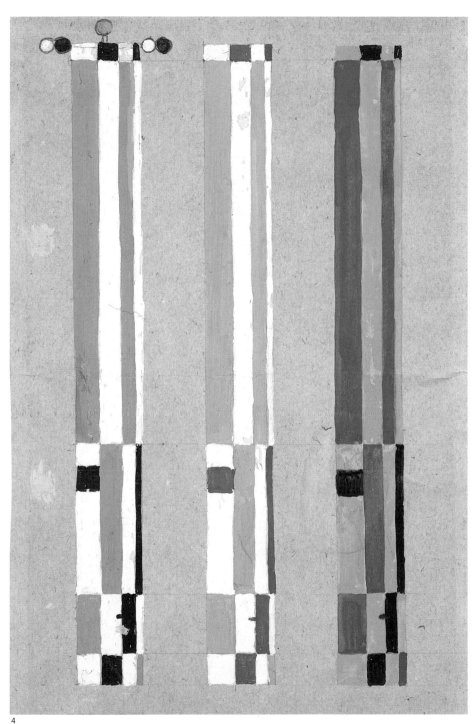

4 **Josef Albers**
Three designs for a
Bauhaus flag, 1923
White gouache,
watercolors and
pencil

4

5 **Herbert Bayer**
Design for a
newspaper kiosk,
1924
Tempera and
collage
Acquired through
the German Class
Lottery Foundation,
Berlin

5

6
László Moholy-Nagy
Cover for the
Bauhaus book 8,
1925
Letterpress print

7 **Herbert Bayer**
Trial new alphabet
From the Bauhaus
special number of
the periodical
"Offset", vol. 7, 1926
Letterpress print

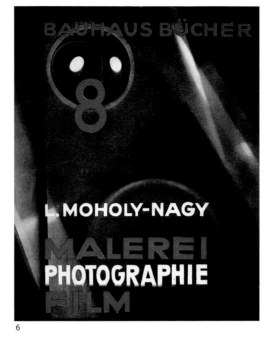

6

HERBERT BAYER: Abb. 1. Alfabet
„g" und „k" sind noch als
unfertig zu betrachten

Beispiel eines Zeichens
in größerem Maßstab
Präzise optische Wirkung

sturm blond

Abb. 2. Anwendung

7

8

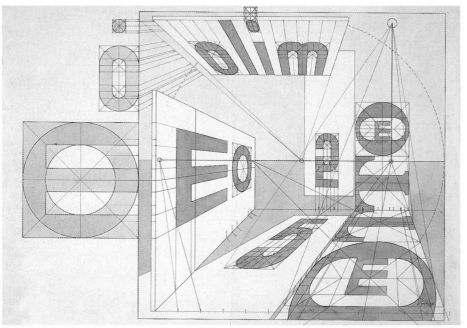

9

8 **Herbert Bayer**
Title page of the
periodical "bauhaus",
vol. 1, 1928
Letterpress print

9 **Erich Mrozek**
Letters in perspective
Exercise from the
class of Joost
Schmidt, 1931
Tempera and
Indian ink

10 **Herbert Bayer**
Poster
"section allemande"
for the exhibition of
the German
Werkbund in Paris,
1930
Color lithograph

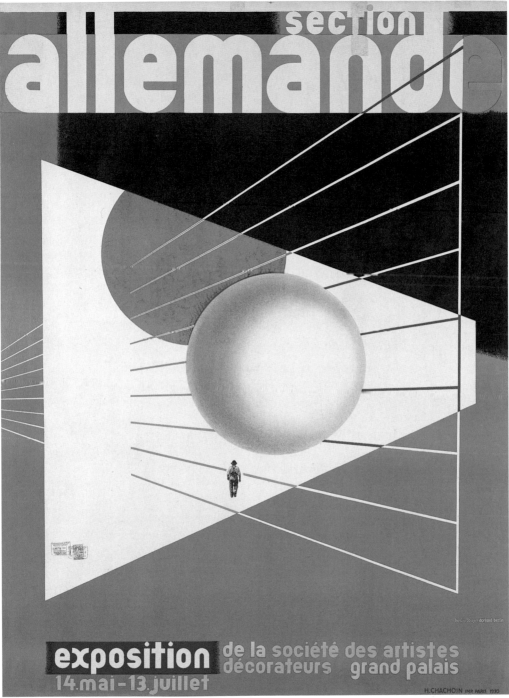

10

Photography at the Bauhaus

At first, photography hardly played a role at the Bauhaus. During the first years, it was not part of the curriculum and, apart from some few exceptions such as with Georg Muche, photography was not used as an independent artistic medium. The decisive impulse for the concern with photography was given by László Moholy-Nagy in 1923. Thence, the wide spectrum of individualistic works developed, produced in the following years by such exceptional photographers as Erich Consemüller, Andreas and T. Lux Feininger, Florence Henri, Lucia Moholy, Walter Peterhans, or Umbo. Also, photographic experiments and amateur shots of many students should not be forgotten.

Based on Russian Avant-garde, photography was, in the eyes of Moholy-Nagy, the ideal creative medium for a "New Vision". He sought in this "pure design of light" new possibilities for the perception and interpretation of a new world, radically transformed by the impact of modern technology. Moholy-Nagy, with the abstract light-pictures of his photograms, his unconventional perspectives and image depiction, the montage and collage techniques, and the multiple exposures, became a pioneer of experimental photography. At the same time, he was one of the first to recognize the value of photography as an instrument for commercial art and advertising. The "Typofoto", a combination of image and text, played a central role in his own publications and then also in the work of Herbert Bayer. In contrast to Moholy-Nagy, who was self-taught, his wife, Lucia Moholy, had been trained in photography. Her aim was less experimental than objective; she was less interested in the game with photographic techniques than in a subtle and unspectacular concern with reality as defined by "New Objectivity". Lucia Moholy's documentary shots of the material produced by the workshops, architecture, and interior spaces, originally meant for use in publications and by the press, as well as her fascinating portraits of masters and students of the Bauhaus, have been decisive in the image making of the school.

It was only with the new curriculum structure under the direction of Hannes Meyer in 1929 that a photography class was founded at the Bauhaus in Dessau under the leadership of Walter Peterhans. Here, the students learned not only photographic theory and practice, but also precise vision. Peterhans' own photographs were unattainable ideal examples: delicately arranged close-up still lifes composed of inconspicuous found objects and fragments of textiles, glass, and metal, of single threads, feathers, and blades of grass. Meticulous lighting catches forms and textures in their finest nuances and imbues them with a near magical effect. His titles open up a further surrealist poetic dimension.

The Bauhaus at Dessau cultivated a lively photographic scene, which was soon to boom. Many of the photographic experiments have been preserved, often even snapshots in which a nonchalant amateurishness can function as creative power. These images have supplied us with details of the everyday life at the Bauhaus, of the work there, the parties, and the optimistic, high-spirited atmosphere of the school.   KW

1 **T. Lux Feininger.** Sport at the Bauhaus, c. 1927, vintage print

2 **László Moholy-Nagy.** Berlin Radio Tower, 1925, vintage print, gift of Sibyl Moholy-Nagy

3 **Lucia Moholy.** Bauhaus building Dessau, Balcony of the studio house, 1926, vintage print, from the estate of the artist

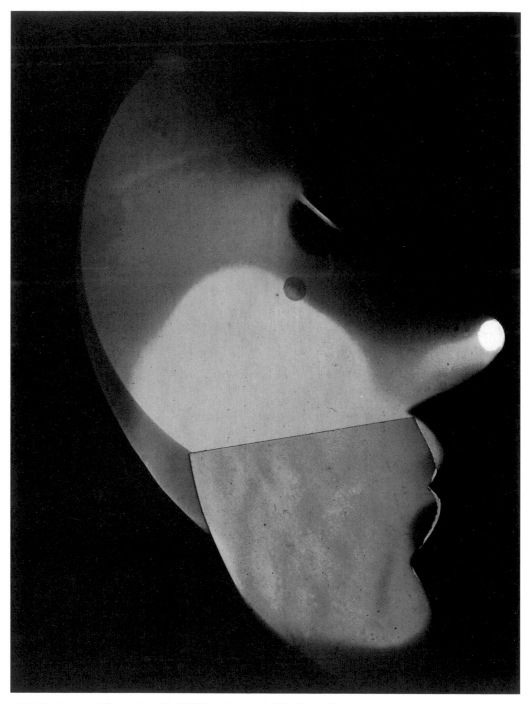

4 **László Moholy-Nagy.** Self portrait in profile, 1925–27, photogram, gift of Sibyl Moholy-Nagy

5 **Marianne Brandt.** me (metal workshop), 1927/28, photocollage, from the estate of Walter Gropius

6

6 **László Moholy-Nagy**
Poster design for
Goerz, 1925
Photogram and
positive print
Gift of Sibyl
Moholy-Nagy

8

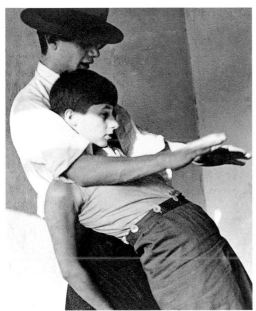

7

7 **Etel Mittag-Fodor**
Albert Mentzel and
Lotte Rothschild,
c. 1930
Vintage print

8 **Andreas Feininger**
Portrait of Lyonel
Feininger, c. 1929
Vintage print

9 **Herbert Bayer**
Bicycle, 1928
Vintage print

9

10

11

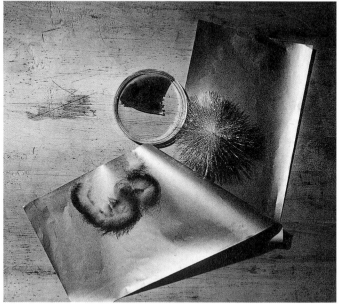

10 **Werner David Feist**
Alarm clock, c. 1929
Vintage print
From the estate of
Walter Gropius

11 **Georg Muche**
Photo-composition,
1921
Enlargement c. 1931
by Lucia Moholy
Vintage print
Gift of Georg Muche

12 **Walter Peterhans**
Dead hare, c. 1929
Vintage print
Gift of Margarete
Leischner

12

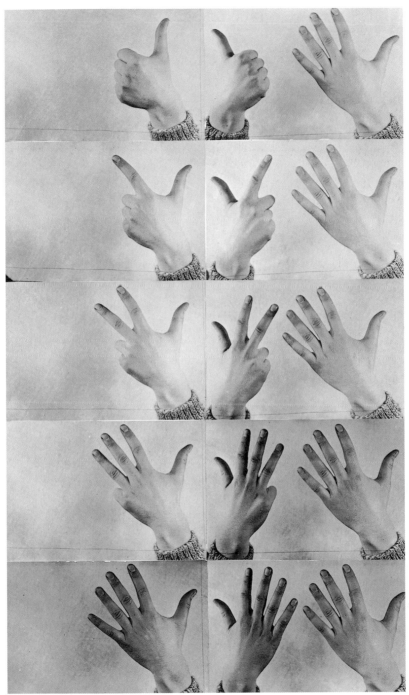

13 **Kurt Kranz**
Numbers signs row,
1930/31
Montage 1970
Vintage prints
Gift of Kurt Kranz

13

The "Light-Space modulator" by László Moholy-Nagy

The "Light-Space modulator" was finally realized in 1930, after many years of preparation and with the help of an engineer and a technician. When, in 1937, he emigrated to the USA, Moholy-Nagy took the original with him. Today it is preserved at the Busch-Reisinger-Museum in Cambridge/Mass. The Bauhaus Archive owns one of two reconstructions.

Moholy-Nagy himself described this kinetic sculpture, this Gesamtkunstwerk composed of color, light, and movement, which appears as a synthesis of his artistic ideas, as an "apparatus for the demonstration of the effects of light and movement". In 1930, the "light-requisite for an electrical stage", such was another description, was exhibited at the show of the German Werkbund in Paris. Moholy-Nagy described it as follows: "The model consists of a cubic box [...] with a circular opening (stage) at the front. Surrounding the opening, on the back side of the board, I have mounted a number of yellow, green, blue, red, and white electrical bulbs [...]. Inside the box, parallel to the front, there is a second board, also with a circular opening, around which a further set of different light bulbs is mounted. Single bulbs light up at different places and intervals according to a pre-set plan. They illuminate a continuously moving mechanism, made partly of transparent, partly of cut-out materials, in order to create linear shadows on the back wall of the closed box. (When the presentation takes place in a dark room, the back wall of the box can be removed and the color and shadow projection behind the box projected on a suitable screen of open dimensions.)"

This is the form the modulator would have had as the central piece in the "Raum der Gegenwart" ("Contemporary Room") in the Provinzialmuseum in Hanover, which Moholy-Nagy had conceived together with the museum's director, Alexander Dorner. The project was never to be realized. In 1930, Moholy-Nagy captured the movement and light effects from his apparatus in the film "Motion picture black-white-grey". In the same year, he wrote: "It is indeed foreseeable that this or similar motion pictures may be transmitted by radio. In part with the support of telescopal prospects, in part as real light plays, whereby the listener owns a private lighting apparatus which can be remotely conducted from the radio station via electrically controlled color filters."   KW

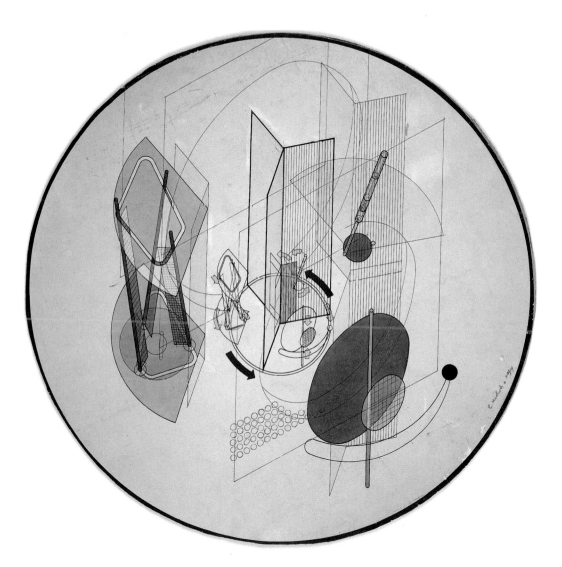

László Moholy-Nagy
The mechanics of
the light-requisite,
1930
Watercolor, Indian
ink, pencil

133

László Moholy-Nagy
Light-Space modulator
(light requisite for
an electrical stage),
1922–1930
Reconstruction 1970
Chrome plated steel,
aluminum, glass,
acrylic glass, wood

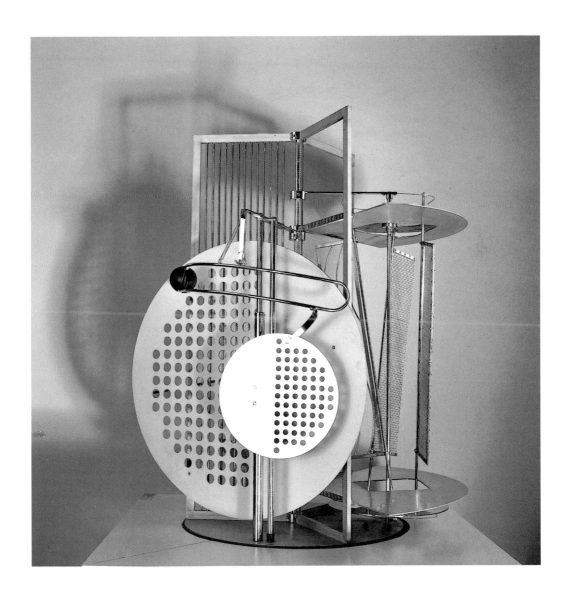

Bauhaus stage

A stage workshop functioned at the Bauhaus from 1921 until 1929. Initially it was headed by Lothar Schreyer, and then by Oskar Schlemmer, from 1923 onwards. Schlemmer called the Bauhaus stage "the meeting point of the metaphysical, in contrast to far too objective tendencies". At other times, he described it as "the flower in the buttonhole of the Bauhaus". This workshop indeed contributed to the development of the Bauhaus from handcrafts to industrial design in a very unique manner.

The expressionist painter and poet Lothar Schreyer planned a Gesamtkunstwerk in which the stage was to be a place of purification and deliverance for the human being. The protagonists acted with pure shapes and colors, often clad in body masks larger than life size, using symbolical movements and sounds. This kind of theater did not gain the approval of the majority of the members of the Bauhaus. An éclat broke out during a rehearsal of the "Mondspiel" (Moonplay), which led Schreyer to resign from his position as head of the stage workshop and to leave the Bauhaus.

Oskar Schlemmer, who then took over the stage workshop, had in the past dedicated considerable time to questions of modern dance. Between 1916 and 1922, he had developed the "Triadic Ballet", a plotless costume play in which the essential features of geometrically stylized body attire defined the dance. On the Bauhaus stage, Schlemmer continued to base his work on the human figure as a model determined by mathematical and geometrical formulae. The stage workshop made masks, costumes, and requisites and studied the mechanical, optical, and acoustic requirements of stage work. The students worked on stage sets, studied movement and representation, and were trained in stage direction, collaborating on productions which took place not only at the Bauhaus, but which also went on tour, securing the school wide publicity.

The most important platform for the Bauhaus stage was the auditorium of the Bauhaus building in Dessau. Schlemmer's "Bauhaus dances" and Kandinsky's "Pictures at an exhibition" to the music of Modest Mussorgsky were performed there. The stage workshop was regularly on the organizing committee of the legendary Bauhaus parties, where the Bauhaus Band also played an important role. During the Hannes Meyer era and after the departure of Schlemmer in 1929, the Bauhaus stage developed its radius of action to political agitation theater.

During their time at the Bauhaus, students like Kurt Schmidt, Xanti Schawinsky, or Heinz Loew regularly contributed sketches, costumes, and theatrical experiments to the theater projects. The Bauhaus stage workshop even produced new ideas on theater architecture, but plans such as the spherical theater by Andor Weininger were never realized.   PH

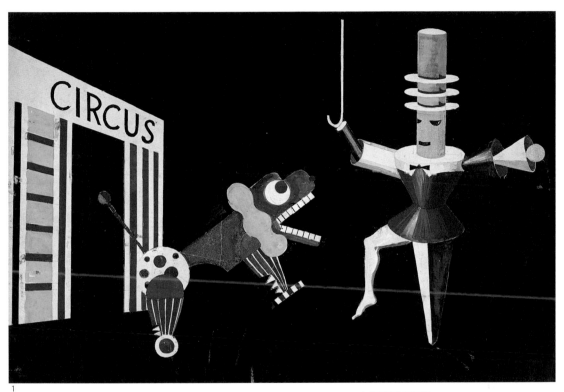

1

1 **Xanti Schawinsky**
Circus, c. 1924
Set design
Tempera, Indian ink,
silverbronze

2 **Lothar Schreyer**
"Mary in the moon"
figurine for
"Moonplay", 1923
Color lithograph

3 **Erich Consemüller**
The building as a
stage, c. 1927
Members of the
stage workshop in
costumes by Oskar
Schlemmer

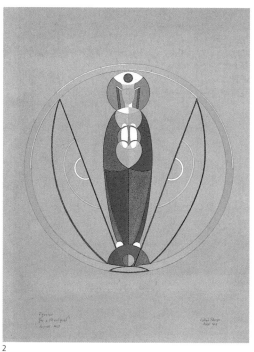

2

3

138

4

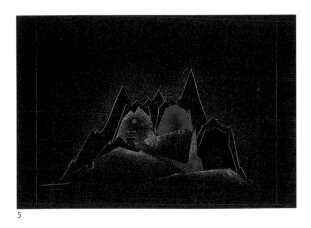

5

4 **Heinz Loew**
Mechanical stage
model, 1927
Reconstruction 1968

5 **Oskar Schlemmer**
Stage set for "The
fortunate hand", 1930
Collage with tempera
and color crayons

139

6

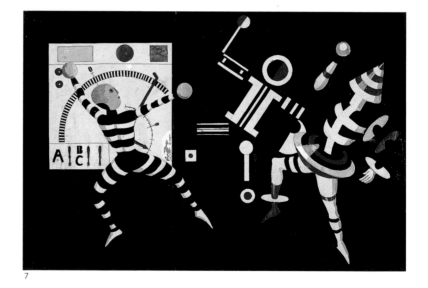

6 **Xanti Schawinsky**
Bauhaus experi-
mental comedia,
c. 1928
Collage with
photographs by
Lux Feininger

7 **Kurt Schmidt**
The man at the
switchboard, c. 1924
Tempera and silver-
bronze on paper

7

140

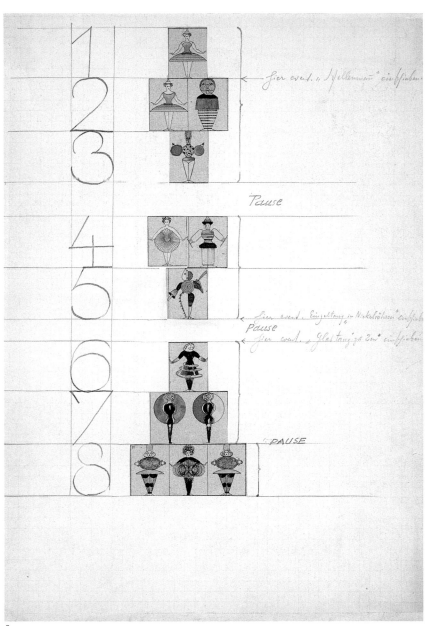

9

9 **Oskar Schlemmer**
Sheet from the
"Triadic ballet"
scenario book, 1927
Collage, watercolor
and pencil

Music and Bauhaus

Despite never having been on the Bauhaus curriculum, music was nevertheless of considerable importance to the school. Some of the most important Bauhaus masters showed a remarkable musical affinity, both in their personal surroundings and in their creative work. Paul Klee, for instance, was a distinguished violin player, and often took recourse in his work to musical analogies; similarly, Lyonel Feininger both painted and composed. Already before taking on his position at the Bauhaus, Vassily Kandinsky had defined the double perception of synaesthetics – the acoustic and optical equivalence between colors, shapes, and tones. His painting also closely relates to music. Johannes Itten's basic courses in pictorial composition attributed a central focus to musical rhythm. It was Itten who attempted to enroll the Viennese composer and music theoretician, Josef Matthias Hauer, involved in the research of a systematic relationship between tone and color, to teach at the Bauhaus. This never came about; Gertrud Grunow's "harmonizing theory", however, together with her concept of a unity of color, form, and tone assured a music-oriented class at the early Bauhaus. The credo of the Bauhaus teachings, from the elementary to a synthesis of the arts, could not omit music.

During the later development of the Bauhaus towards industrial design, the free artistic attitude of the initial years was reduced. The inclination towards a Gesamtkunstwerk with the necessary inclusion of elements of music, however, remained effective. László Moholy-Nagy's stage concept coordinated form, movement, light, color, tone, and the human being to a "theater of totality" (1925). Before him, Oskar Schlemmer, Vassily Kandinsky, and Lothar Schreyer had already postulated similar intentions. Musical aspirations could best be articulated within the capacities of the stage workshop. Bauhaus students carried out experiments with light modulators for color and form, some of them tried their hands at composition (i.e. Ludwig Hirschfeld-Mack). Others, under the influence of Kandinsky, tried out new forms of transcription for the translation of musical structures into visual compositions (i.e. Heinrich Bormann and Heinrich Neugeboren). The students of the Bauhaus Band contributed to the lightness of Bauhaus social life, and were accordingly very appreciated by the public: at first they worked with a tonality originating in Eastern Europe, later with jazz-like improvisations. Last but not least, there was a special Bauhaus whistle tone for a musical identification between members of the school.

The educational concept of the Bauhaus was universal; accordingly, it rejected early specialization and a strict separation between the artistic disciplines. Musical events therefore had their place parallel to the professional classes, and the students were familiar with both classical programs and contemporary compositions. Here, famous artists such as Rudolf Serkin, Adolf Busch, and Arthur Schnabel were involved. A special event was the "Bauhaus week" of 1923, during which Hermann Scherchen directed concerts with works of Schönberg, Krenek, Weill, Busoni, Hindemith, and Stravinsky. In 1926, Eduard Erdmann was invited by Walter Gropius to play at the inauguration of the new Bauhaus building, and the auditorium was often used in subsequent years for concerts and lectures on musical themes.   PH

1 Program sheet
for a lieder recital
by Emmy Heim,
1921

2 Program sheet
for the "Bauhaus
week", 1923

3 Score for the
Bauhaus whistle,
c, 1923

1

2

3

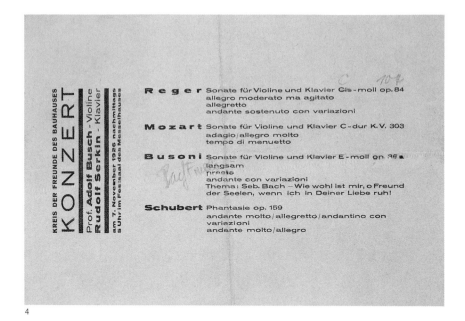

4

5

6

4 Program sheet for
a concert organized
by the Circle of
Friends of the
Bauhaus, 1927

5 **T. Lux Feininger**,
Oskar Schlemmer as
a musical clown
Photograph, 1928

6 Bauhaus band
flyer, c. 1931

7

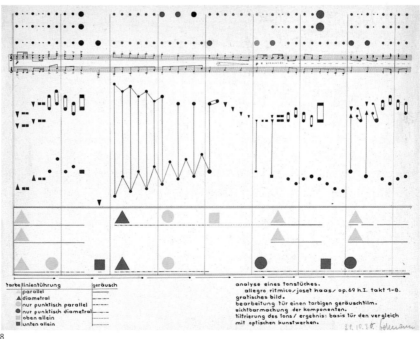

8

7 Poster for the
Eduard Erdmann
evening piano
concert, 1931

8 Heinrich Bormann
Analysis of a piece
of music, 1930
From Kandinsky's
class

Wall painting

Today, the Bauhaus wall painting workshop has almost been forgotten.

In retrospect, the early interior decoration schemes for villas carried out by the workshop are difficult to classify. The choice of colors and the finish of the design neither correspond with later works, nor do they reflect our general knowledge of color style in the twenties: it is not unusual for very dark sections of a room to contrast with quite light areas. The pastel color range was, at the time, quite common for villas; primary colors remain absent. Rooms are defined as closed entities, with no attempt to combine different spaces in a related structure.

Vassily Kandinsky's appointment as master of form focused the interest of the workshop on large-scale mural paintings independent in composition from the actual wall. Kandinsky's room at the Jury-free Art Exhibition in Berlin in 1922 and Oskar Schlemmer's murals in Weimar are seminal pieces within this development.

The late Weimar years and the early Dessau period led to a return to architecture-related decoration. Some designs try to structure rooms with color accents, to highlight specific surfaces and to create defined areas within one room with the support of color. Walls and ceilings are dealt with as a single color unit.

Hinnerk Scheper, head of the workshop since 1925, developed a contrasting concept of decoration at the service of architecture. He avoided choosing bright colors and instead used light pastel tones, backed-up by a wide palette of grays. Color differentiation was such that structural elements of the architecture were emphasized through color rather than encroached upon. Scheper never worked against existing architecture. His approach is marked by the rules of workmanship, inseparably bound to a strong sense of the effect of color. Scheper worked on the base of color charts; these, however, could be adapted at any time if, in situ, the desired effect was not attainable. This discreet attitude enabled him to take on restoration work on historical buildings.

His classes, which finally ran under the title "color", were strongly oriented towards craftsmanship. He demanded that a sophisticated color tone scale for oil painting be devised, and laid great importance on the command of different techniques of color shading such as spraying and screening. He considered a founded knowledge of the different components of colors to be just as indispensable as professional know-how in various kinds of rough-casting materials.

Despite this focus on craftsman design, the Bauhaus wallpaper was developed in 1929 as an industrial product. Made for apartments in contemporary housing estates, the patterns were kept small and subdued in tone. The wallpaper was so well-adapted to its specific function that it became the most successful Bauhaus product. CW

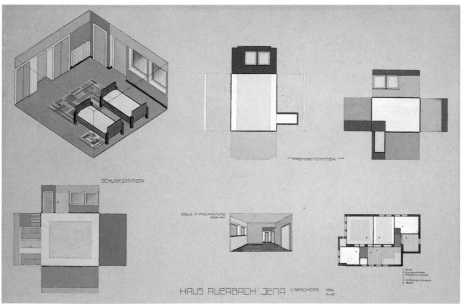

1

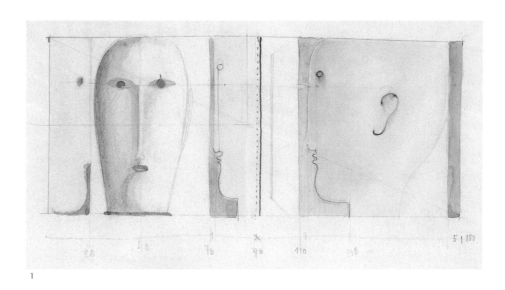

1 **Oskar Schlemmer**
Head frieze, 1923
Sketch for a mural
painting in the
apartment of
Adolf Meyer
Watercolor, pencil,
pen and ink on
tracing paper

2 **Alfred Arndt**
Color plan for the
Auerbach house in
Iena, 1924
Tempera and Indian
ink on drawing
paper

2

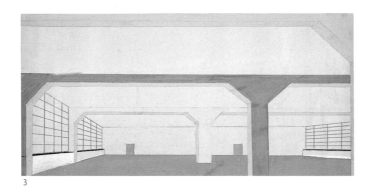

3

3 **Lothar Lang**
Design for a color
scheme in the
workshop wing of
the Dessau Bauhaus,
1926
Indian ink and tem-
pera on cardboard

4 **Hinnerk Scheper**
Trial design of a
color scheme for the
Dessau Bauhaus,
1926
Tempera on photo-
print

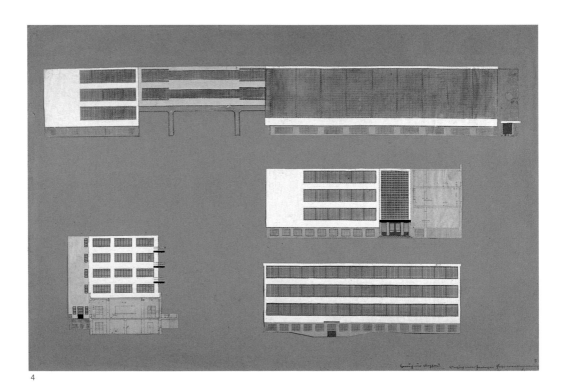

4

5a

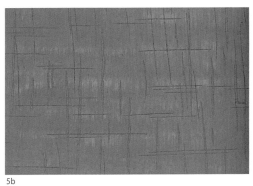
5b

5a/b
Bauhaus wallpaper
Samples from the
first collection, 1929

6 **Pius Pahl**
Color study for
house C, 1931/32
Tempera over
pencil on drawing
paper
Gift Pius Pahl

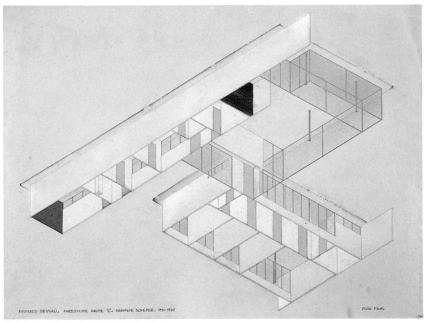

6

Architecture and architecture classes with Walter Gropius 1919–1927

The early Bauhaus had to live with the paradox that, although its founding manifesto called for "building", the school didn't offer any classes in architecture. The courses closest to architecture were represented by material drawing.

When, despite this situation, architecture tuition indeed became available, it was only because Walter Gropius readily accepted that his partner Adolf Meyer took on students in his private office and worked with them in the classical relationship of master and journeyman on the basis of commissions which came in. Various attempts at introducing regular architecture courses were short-lived. It was only in the very last semester at Weimar that Adolf Meyer led a course; the number of participants, however, was limited.

The buildings of Gropius and Meyer were, in many ways, "Bauhaus buildings". Throughout his lectures and publications, Gropius made no distinction between private and school commissions. He regularly let students work on the commissions in his office and always tried to sell products and services from the Bauhaus workshops to his clients. Gropius never saw any conflict of interest in this system: The architecture of the Bauhaus was the architecture of the school's director. This form of collaboration resulted in famous projects: The house of Adolf Sommerfeld in Berlin, a builder and patron of the Bauhaus, the alteration of the theater in Jena (both destroyed), the Otte house in Berlin, and the Auerbach house in Jena. The competition design for the Chicago Tribune led the Gropius office to international fame.

Only very few student projects outside the office of Gropius are known: the most important one is the planning of a housing estate for members of the Bauhaus. The first plans from around 1920 foresaw an ensemble of wooden houses, the material of the time. In 1922/23, masters and students developed other forms of housing in which the central living space was located in the middle of the building. Here, not only new techniques and materials were tested, but also new design principles as introduced to Weimar by Theo van Doesburg. Such a house was realized for the Bauhaus exhibition of 1923 after a design by Georg Muche. Adolf Meyer assured the building's realization. The Bauhaus workshops fully equipped the "experimental house am Horn". The architecture was far less radical than the interior decoration, which was intended to convey very specific ideas regarding the changed lifestyle of "New Man".

These rudiments were further developed during the following years. In particular, Marcel Breuer avoided the visible compromise in the exhibition house between an overall traditional concept and a modern elevation; he developed his designs against existing conventions. They were not carried out within the context of real building projects, and can only be rated as freely chosen projections into a building future, surpassing by far the designs from the Gropius/Meyer office. The looseness of the ties in the atmosphere at the Bauhaus in Weimar was extremely beneficial to this kind of school of thought. CW

1 **Walter Gropius
und Adolf Meyer**
Skyscraper for the
"Chicago Tribune",
1922
Indian ink and gray
wash on paper

1

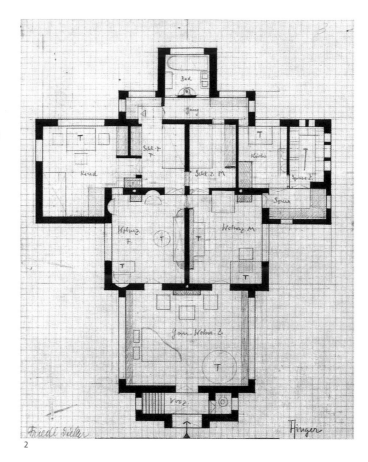

2 **Friedl Dicker und Franz Singer**
Design for a detached house, 1921/22
Indian ink and pencil on graph paper

3 **Lothar Schreyer**
Design for a detached house, c. 1922
Pencil on graph paper

2

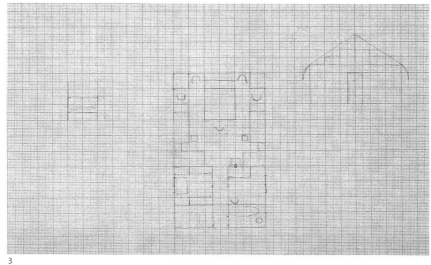

3

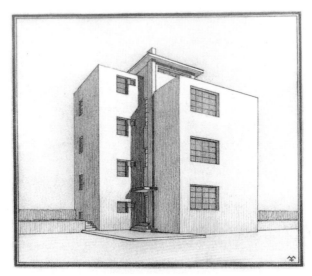

4

4 **Fred Forbat**
Design for a studio
house Am Horn,
Weimar, 1922/23
Pencil on tracing
paper

5 **Marcel Breuer**
Maquette for an
apartment house,
1924
Contemporary
photograph

5

Bauhaus buildings in Dessau

The move of the Bauhaus from Weimar to Dessau not only assured the continuation of the school – the town also enabled it to erect its own building. Gropius saw this as an opportunity to articulate his ideas of a reformed art school in the medium of architecture.

He developed a complex of different bodies of architecture whose individual design was meant to reflect each particular usage. Following the requirements postulated by Gropius, the individual units of the complex are carefully related to one another both in volume and in height, such that the design of the entire building could still be identified from an airplane or a balloon.

On a plot of land situated on the outskirts of town, Gropius tried to do away with old forms of representation by developing a strategy of differentiated façades assigned to the individual building units. Although the area surrounding the building plot was mainly undeveloped, Gropius succeeded in making the visitor walk around the complex in order to obtain a general idea of the building; no single standpoint enabled the viewer to grasp all the different units with their specific functions.

At the same time, a small housing estate was built for the Bauhaus masters in a pine-tree grove close by. Their exterior appearance was closely related to that of the school building. Each master installed and painted the inside of his house according to his own personal taste. The individually designed interiors provided an example of the potentials offered by these spaces to be different depending on the use of color and furniture.

On the inauguration of the Bauhaus building in Dessau, the stonework for 60 apartments in the housing estate of Törten was finished. For years, Gropius had been studying the challenge of building low-cost residential complexes. His aim was to industrialize construction, with cranes and cement-mixers replacing trowels and bricks. He designed new ground plans and, due to unavoidable errors in experimental building, didn't only harvest compliments from the inhabitants. The "standard" propagated by Gropius was not to be found in these rows of semi-detached houses.

His last commission in Dessau was the Arbeitsamt (labor office), a new type of building for those days. The major architectural problem was the requirement for the rapid and efficient channelling of large groups of people through the building. Gropius met the task in designing a single-level, semi-circular building, whose entrance, exit, and inner organization were meant to support the assistance delivered to the unemployed. This ambition was fulfilled at the beginning of 1929, when the number of unemployed was still relatively low.

Gropius had always been conscious of the impact of publications. Part of his work consisted in the personal choice of photographs best suited for relating his intentions. This was very much the case for the buildings in Dessau: his controlled practice of publishing images of the school precincts has formed the image of the Bauhaus for generations of admirers and art historians. Today, it is not the real building, but rather the published image that is most representative of it. This is why we also only publish the historical photographs.

CW

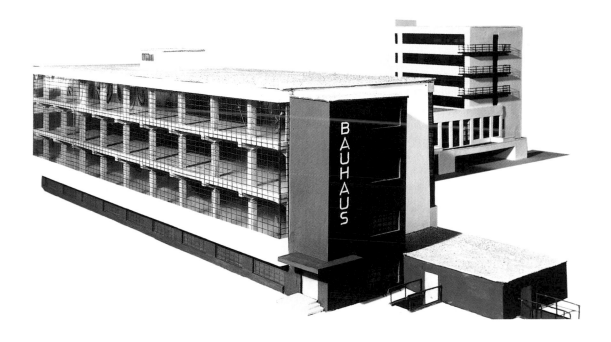

1 **Walter Gropius**
Bauhaus building:
original maquette,
1925
Gift Museum of
Modern Art,
New York

2

3

2 **Walter Gropius**
Bauhaus building:
studio house, from
the Southeast, 1927
Photo:
Erich Consemüller

3 **Walter Gropius**
Bauhaus building:
workshop unit,
connecting bridge,
and school build-
ing, from the
Southwest, 1926/27
Photo:
Lucia Moholy

4 **Walter Gropius**
Bauhaus building:
entire complex by
night, from the
Northwest, 1926

4

156

5

6

5 **Walter Gropius**
Gropius' master
house, from the
Southeast, 1926
Photo:
Lucia Moholy

6 **Walter Gropius**
Semi-detached
master houses,
from the
Northwest, 1926
Photo:
Lucia Moholy

157

7

8

7 **Walter Gropius**
Labor office Dessau
Bird's-eye perspec-
tive of the semi-
circular building
Maquette (1986,
GDR Building
Academy)

8 **Walter Gropius**
Labor office Dessau
View of the
Southern elevation,
1929
Photo: Theis

9

10

9 **Walter Gropius**
Törten housing
estate: positioning
of ceiling rafts with
the help of a crane
Stills from the
Humboldt film
1928

10 **Walter Gropius**
Törten housing
estate
View of the estate,
1928
Photo: Theis

159

Building studies with Hannes Meyer 1927–1930

In 1927, Hannes Meyer was appointed director of architectural tuition. His building studies were based on three fundamental assumptions:
• All courses in architecture must be based on scientific facts. Major priority is given to the functionalism of a building in the most practical sense. Any elaboration of a design must therefore be preceded by research on the usage, from which the building program should be developed with scientific precision;
• The optimization of all necessary requirements has priority over artistic considerations;
• All courses in architecture must be based on activities from architectural practice.

The theoretical section of the course concentrated with great intensity on studies in usage and reasoning, the results of which were documented in diagrams, so as to demonstrate the scientific approach. Establishing planning documents diverged from common practice in Germany, where schooling was still based on "major" commission work, such as town halls, libraries, and theaters. Meyer considered building to be pure organization, void of any creative component. The exterior of these designs, with their angular appearance and poor in detail, in which each element can be "accounted for", not only tried to break with traditional building aesthetics, but also attempted to make the design principles of New Architecture, with their emphasis on equilibrium and rhythm, seem overhauled.

The correlation to building practice was secured by Meyer in a commission by the town of Dessau for four Laubenganghäuser (loggia apartment buildings). Planning and realization were both entirely in the hands of the building department at the Bauhaus. The buildings were conceived with rented apartments, reachable via an open-air exterior corridor. The habitations were designed with two or two and a half rooms – a form of living that, in theory, had many positive aspects, but was usually rejected by the tenants.

The building department was also called upon by Meyer for the construction of his design for the house of the Federal School of the German Trade Unions (ADGB) in Bernau, near Berlin. In a preliminary stage, all functions which the building was to fulfill were subject to research; their translation into architecture was the logical conclusion of the study. Meyer accounted for the general disposition of the floor plan with pedagogical imperatives of communal life; some ideological elements, however, together with the proportions of the whole complex, make us wonder as to the supposed nonconsideration of aesthetic values.

Despite high building standards regarding both the interior and the exterior, the construction has quite a parsimonious appearance. This impression was certainly intended in order to avoid comparison with feudal buildings; the idea was to develop a form of architecture specific to the working class. The building was principally equipped with pre-tested industrial products; the Bauhaus workshops were commissioned with special tasks. In contrast to many other modern buildings, the various architectural masses of the Federal School were ideally suited to blend in with the surrounding wooded landscape. CW

1 **Hannes Meyer, Hans Wittwer and the building department of the Dessau Bauhaus** Federal School of the German Trade Unions (ADGB), in Bernau near Berlin, 1928–30 Maquette (1989, GDR Building Academy)

161

2

3

2 **Hannes Meyer,
Hans Wittwer, and
building depart-
ment of the Dessau
Bauhaus**
Federal School of
the German Trade
Unions (ADGB) in
Bernau near Berlin,
1928–30
View from the
South

3 **Hannes Meyer,
Hans Wittwer, and
building depart-
ment of the Dessau
Bauhaus**
Federal School of
the German Trade
Unions (ADGB) in
Bernau near Berlin,
1928–30
View from the West

Photos:
Walter Peterhans

4

4 **Hannes Meyer, Hans Wittwer, and building department of the Dessau Bauhaus** Federal School of the German Trade Unions (ADGB) in Bernau near Berlin Northern view of the pavilions with canteen pergola garden in the foreground, 1928–30

5

5 **Hannes Meyer, Hans Wittwer, and building department of the Dessau Bauhaus** Federal School of the German Trade Unions (ADGB) in Bernau near Berlin Reading room adjacent to the library

6 **Hannes Meyer, Hans Wittwer, and building department of the Dessau Bauhaus** Federal School of the German Trade Unions (ADGB) in Bernau near Berlin Glass passageway between the main building, the residential quarters, and the gymnasium, 1928–30

Photos: Walter Peterhans

6

Urban planning seminars with Ludwig Hilberseimer 1929–1933

Hannes Meyer appointed new teachers at the Bauhaus for his building studies. Most important of all was Ludwig Hilberseimer, an urban planner who had made himself a name with a number of publications on New Building and who had specialized in private housing and housing estates. His classes revolved around various types of small apartments and the organization of housing estates as urban planning projects. He particularly favored mixed-height housing developments, with high-rise apartment buildings for singles and couples without children and bungalows with gardens for families.

An ever-recurring object of study was the L-shaped bungalow for a small family that was ideal for an adaptation to the sun's orientation and, in addition, easy to enlarge in the case of additional children. The plan and the exterior appearance were both kept very simple in order to allow for different techniques of construction. Also, this type of building enabled the construction of terrace rows on small plots of land. The hope was that in this way, higher building expenses could be compensated.

The American model of high-rise apartment buildings was taken as the ideal for singles and couples without children. It was assumed of the inhabitants that they were extremely mobile, would own a limited amount of possessions, and even, ideally, could "live out of a suitcase". Since communal services such as restaurants and laundry facilities were available, it was thought that both the size of the apartments and their furnishings could be substantially reduced. This left little option for a personal touch in the arrangement of the space. The apartment buildings were laid out according to accents in height within a general urban concept.

Urban planning analysis in the classroom resulted in projects for the restructuring of entire cities, such as Dessau, or of single districts, such as Berlin-Mitte. The aim was to create a new type of city while avoiding all known and existing drawbacks. Not only was the new city supposed to be a social ideal, it was also hoped that it would be of such incomparable economic benefit that an urge to transform existing cities would inevitably ensue. They were divided into clearly arranged units, where industrial areas were separated from living quarters, but remained well-connected to them by suitable service roads. Major traffic crossroads were surrounded by administrative buildings, business, and cultural centers.

Hilberseimer's theory was based on a closed system of thought developed out of the rejection of the nineteenth-century city, from the individual bungalow to general urban planning. Only very little influence from reform ideas developed in Germany after 1910 can be traced in his highly individual visions.   CW

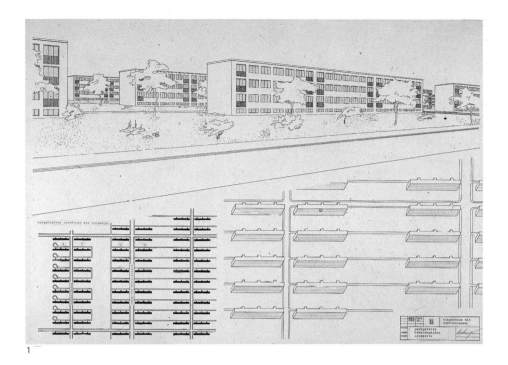

1

1 **Eduard Ludwig**
House on different
levels with apart-
ments towards the
South, 1931
Perspective view,
plot plan, and
isometric view
Indian ink on paper

2 **Pius Pahl**
Chain building with
terrace rows open
to extension,
1931/32
Ground plans and
elevation views
Indian ink on
drawing paper
Gift of Pius Pahl

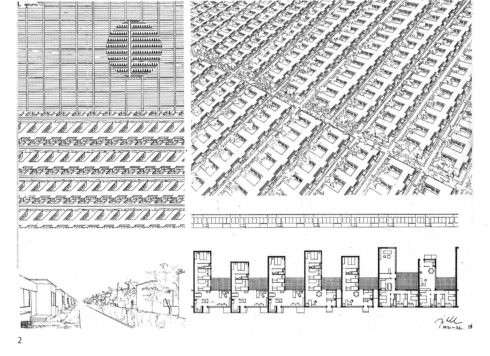

2

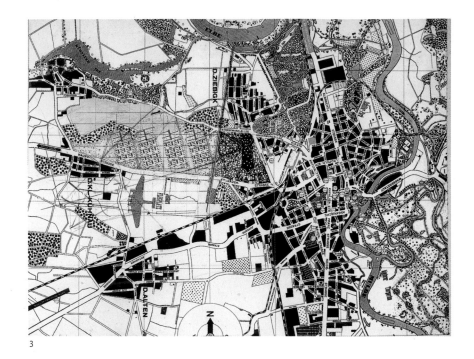

3

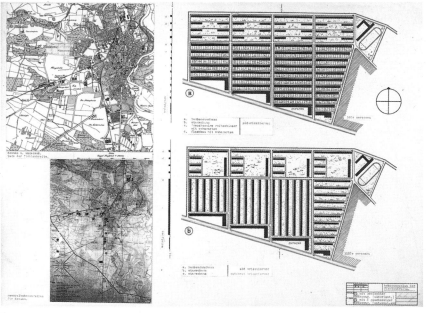

4

3 **Wilhelm Jakob Hess, Cornelius van der Linden**
Laborer's housing estate for Junkers, 1931
Site plan in scale with the area of Dessau
Collage on printed town map
Gift Wilhelm Jakob Hess

4 **Eduard Ludwig**
Building project for Fichtenbreite, 1931
Collage and Indian ink on drawing paper

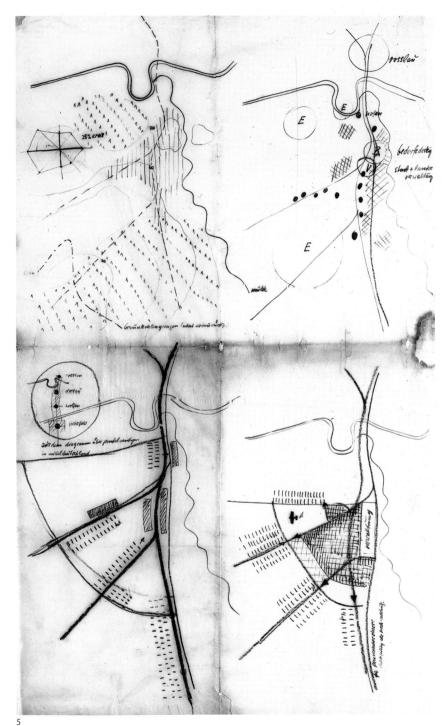

5 **Wils Ebert**
Sketches for a
restructuring of
Dessau, c. 1931
upper left: natural
conditions and
wind diagram
upper right:
distribution of
industrial, domestic,
and commercial
districts
lower left:
Restructuring of
circulation
infrastructure and
diagram of
traffic flow
lower right: new
repartition of
domestic and
commercial districts
including
administration
Ink and color pencil
on tracing paper
From the estate of
Wils Ebert

5

Architecture classes with Mies van der Rohe 1930–1933

The appointment of Ludwig Mies van der Rohe as director of the Bauhaus, following the summary dismissal of Hannes Meyer, was programmatic: It was expected of him to reconcile Bauhaus patrons with the institution, to continue with the reforms introduced by Meyer (whereby the economic crisis at the beginning of the thirties necessarily involved restructuring the curriculum), and to present a new Bauhaus image, particularly in architecture.

The tuition system developed by Mies was a reflection of his personal experience; the first step was the acquisition of a solid knowledge in building techniques. This was followed by studies on building types, and finally by designs in urban planning. Mies reserved the last semesters for his own classes. His personal architectural language represented the base of his theories. Solutions to the tasks he confronted the students with were always to be found in his works; the pupils were expected to grasp and understand the unwritten rules of structure and design. Mies considered it better to offer models which could be further worked on in class, rather than to leave the students on their own with a method. The central object of his tuition was a detached family house. He was of the opinion that "whoever can develop such a house correctly has a command over any other architecture".

His definition of function, however, was neither narrow nor scientifically exact, and certainly not subordinated to aesthetic principles. The usage and design of a house were to be combined in order to satisfy both expectations. Mies avoided organizing the life of the inhabitants of his houses right until the last detail in order to minimize the inside surface of the apartments; he created incompara-bly qualitative spaces in which spatial freedom could be experienced. Their impact seems to derive from the preponderance of the architectural form; according to Mies, this indeed was an indispensable regulating power. His elevated ideals in the realm of abstract design could not, in its pure form, be adopted by a curriculum. Mies was conscious of the difficulty in teaching such content. This is why he attached great importance not only to the schooling of the performing hand, but also of the mind, without which the realization of a seemingly simple, yet in reality highly complex idea was impossible.

Mies' architecture was very attractive to students who had concluded their technical education in building and wished to further their aesthetic studies with him. The decision to enroll in the architecture classes at the Bauhaus in 1930/31 can be regarded as a conscious vote for Mies and the aesthetic program that his name stood for. It is therefore not in the least surprising to find many designs amongst the students' works that use his forms as models and work with his running projects. His best students were able to perceive his intentions and to master an aesthetic vocabulary which was universally applicable. Many of his students remained true to him throughout their lives.   CW

1

1 **Ludwig Mies van der Rohe**
Competition entry for a skyscraper at Friedrichstraße railway station, perspective view, 1921
Photography, reworked in diverse techniques

169

2 **Ernst Hegel**
Floor plans for
court houses
Private class with
Mies van der Rohe,
1934
Pencil on tracing
paper
Gift of Ernst Hegel

3 **Ludwig Mies
van der Rohe**
Corrective sketches
concerning a piece
by Wilhelm Jakob
Hess, 1932
Pencil on paper
Gift of Wilhelm
Jakob Hess

4 **Pius Pahl**
House C: garden
elevation, 1931/32
Indian ink on
drawing paper
Gift of Pius Pahl

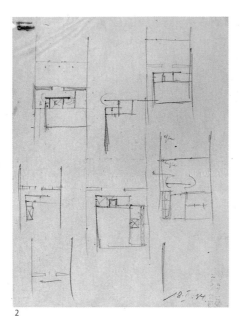

2

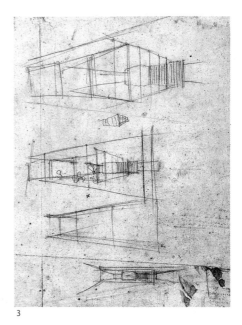

3

4

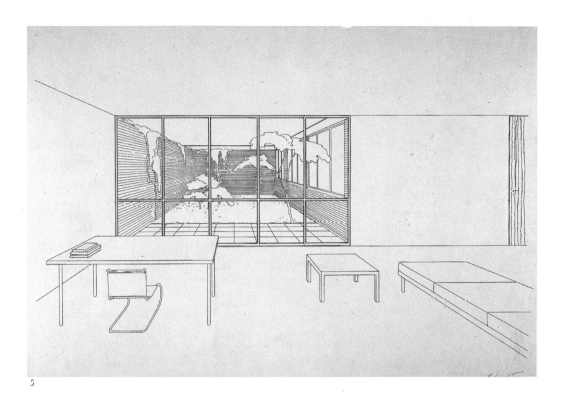

5

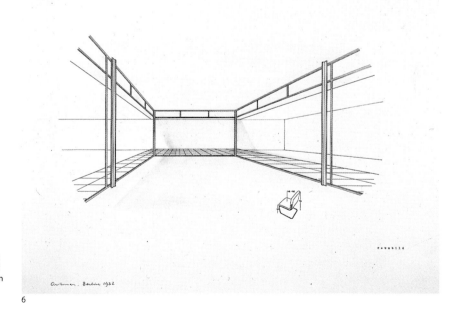

5 **Eduard Ludwig**
Flat building with
living quarters in
a patio, 1930
Indian ink on
drawing paper

6 **Rudolf Ortner**
One room house:
space study, 1932
Indian ink drawing
with application of
catalogue image on
drawing paper

6

171

Bauhaus during National Socialism
1933–1945

Even prior to 1933, the Bauhaus had been defamed by the rising NS movement as "cultural bolshevism"; the controversy continued after the closure of the Bauhaus. An affiliation with the Bauhaus was not in itself grounds enough for persecution, but in many cases led to drastic professional disadvantages. Some of the prominent members of the Bauhaus were already leaving Germany in 1933: Vassily Kandinsky, calumniated as a communist, emigrated to Paris; Paul Klee, under similar accusation, was dismissed from his teaching position in Düsseldorf and left for Switzerland; likewise Josef Albers, together with his wife Anni, followed a call to the USA. Both Gropius and Mies van der Rohe attempted to continue working in Germany before their respective emigrations in 1934 and 1938. Oskar Schlemmer, Gerhard Marcks, and Georg Muche, although removed from office, remained in the country. This was also the case for most of the Bauhaus students, whose respective professional situations during the Nazi years were, however, of quite individual nature.

The architects who had received their education at the Bauhaus were able to seek work in three main fields: exhibition architecture, industrial architecture, and the private sector. Industrial construction represented the only building assignment the Nazis believed suited to a modern language of form. They considered that both representative architectural projects and housing estates should be planned either in a monumental classicist or in a vernacular, regional style. It is within this domain that many of the architecture students from Mies van der Rohe's classes were active, in the enormous Rimpl office complex, for instance, or with the Deutsche Reichspost (postal services of the German Reich). Modern architecture was allowed only in moderation, or confined to rear façades and interiors in the private sector.

The Bauhaus also delivered a terrifying example of the relationship between modern rationalism and systematic extermination: the Canadian historian van Perlt revealed that Fritz Ertl, graduate holder of a Bauhaus Diploma, contributed to the planning of the concentration camp in Auschwitz.

Many of the designers were able to adapt well and with success to the new system, even if "privately" they were against National Socialism: Wilhelm Wagenfeld became the most prominent Bauhaus designer in the position of artistic director of the Vereinigte Lausitzer Glaswerke (United Lausitz Glassworks), and Herbert Bayer's work in the Dorland advertising agency was crowned with success. The communist circles produced a number of opponents to the regime, among whom were the photographer Willi Jungmittag and the KPD member Josef Knau. Jungmittag was murdered in 1944 in the penitentiary of Brandenburg for being a member of an opposition group. Knau fought for three years in the Spanish Civil War, was finally interned in France, and then delivered to the Gestapo. He died as a prisoner aboard the ship "Thielbeck" when it was sunk in the last days of the war.

A memorial plaque at the Bauhaus Archive commemorates the families of the Bauhaus members persecuted during the Nazi period.   MD

1

2

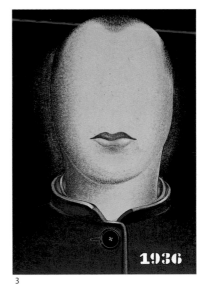

3

1 **Walter Gropius**
Design for a new
"Reichsbank" build-
ing, Berlin, 1933

2 **Herbert Bayer**
Cover illustration
for "die neue linie"
("the new line"),
February 1936
Color print

3 **Franz Ehrlich**
Faceless portrait,
1936
Page 25 from the
series "detention in
Buchenwald"

Bauhaus in exile

In 1933, the development of the Bauhaus in its land of origin was interrupted. As a consequence, many members, amongst them the most prominent ones, left the country. This exile represented a successful continuation of the ideas and program of the Bauhaus.

The former directors Walter Gropius and Ludwig Mies van der Rohe left Germany in 1934 and 1938 respectively. Since 1930 – the year of his dismissal from the Bauhaus – Hannes Meyer, together with a group of students, was active in the Soviet Union, where they participated in urban development projects. Some members of this group were murdered under Stalinist repression or, as in the case of Philipp Tolziner, spent long years in the "Gulag". Some left immediately in 1933 for Western Europe, such as Vassily Kandinsky (France) and Paul Klee (Switzerland). In 1937 and 1938, Lyonel Feininger and Johannes Itten returned to their countries of birth (USA and Switzerland). Many students had to leave Nazi Germany as well for political or "racial" reasons.

The most important destination of the Bauhaus exodus, however, was the USA. Next to Gropius and Mies van der Rohe, the former masters Josef Albers, Marcel Breuer, László Moholy-Nagy, and Herbert Bayer, all close members of the Gropius circle at the Bauhaus, opted for the other side of the Atlantic. Professional rather than political reasons were the motor for the decision to emigrate, together with the belief that a better chance for the realization of their artistic credos could be found outside of Germany. These expectations were to be fulfilled, the former Bauhaus staff finding favorable ground in the United States for a continuation of its work.

A key event as to the impact of the Bauhaus in American exile took place in 1938 with the exhibition "Bauhaus 1919–1928" at the Museum of Modern Art in New York. The time span of the exhibition was confined to the Gropius era; according to Alfred H. Barr, however, the museum's director at the time, the show made an extraordinary impression and paved the way for the progression of the Bauhaus and its members in America. Herbert Bayer, who had designed the show, became a most influential graphic designer; Marcel Breuer likewise followed a successful career as an architect. Not only did Josef Albers work as a respected art teacher at Black Mountain College – a kind of successor to the Bauhaus – and later at Yale University, he became one of the founders of Op Art. Anni Albers built up an exceptional reputation as a weaver. The only design school to carry on the name was the "New Bauhaus", called to life in 1937 by László Moholy-Nagy.   PH

1 **Andreas Feininger** The "Queen Elizabeth" in New York, photograph c. 1951

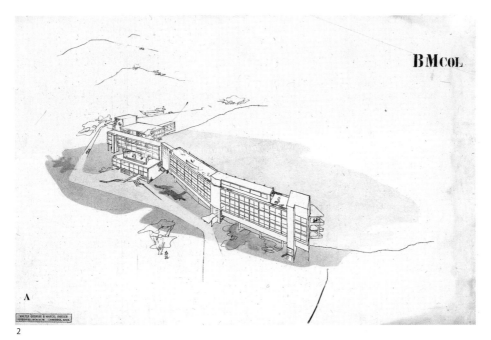

2

3

4

2 **Walter Gropius
and Marcel Breuer**
Black Mountain
College project,
1938/39
General view

3 **Walter Allner**
Cover design for the
magazine "Fortune",
1954
Trial proof

4 **Herbert Bayer**
"Harper's Bazaar"
magazine cover,
August 1940

5 **Walter and
Ise Gropius**
Bauhaus 1919–1928
Book published on
the occasion of the
exhibition at the
Museum of Modern
Art, New York 1938.
Cover design by
Herbert Bayer after a
photograph by
T. Lux Feininger

5

New Bauhaus Chicago

The New Bauhaus, founded in 1937 in Chicago, was the immediate successor to the Bauhaus dissolved in 1933 under National Socialist pressure. Bauhaus ideology had a strong impact throughout America, but it was only at the New Bauhaus that the complete curriculum as developed under Walter Gropius in Weimar and Dessau was adopted and further developed.

The former Bauhaus master László Moholy-Nagy was founding director of the New Bauhaus. He then headed the resulting School of Design from 1938 until his death in 1946 (entitled Institute of Design from 1944 onwards) aiming at liberating the creative potential of his students through disciplined experimentation with materials, techniques, and forms. This corresponded to the preliminary course at the "old Bauhaus", the practice of which was continued, as was a strict affiliation with the workshops during the entire training course. The focus on natural and human sciences was increased, and photography grew to play a more prominent role at the school in Chicago than it had in Germany.

The New Bauhaus therefore offered a "preliminary course" which later ran under the name of "foundation course". In "basic design", the students became familiar with a wide variety of materials (wood, veneer, plastics, textiles, metal, glass, plaster etc.) in order to master their structure, their surface qualities, and their range of application. Training in mechanical techniques was more sophisticated than it had been in Germany.

Emerging from the basic course, various workshops were installed, such as "light, photography, film, publicity", "textile, weaving, fashion", "wood, metal, plastics", "color, painting, decorating" and "architecture". The most important achievement at the Chicago Bauhaus was probably in photography, under the guidance of teachers such as György Kepes, Nathan Lerner, Arthur Siegel or Harry Callahan.

Whereas, in addition to Moholy-Nagy, Hin Bredendieck and Marli Ehrmann, it was initially other emigrants from the Bauhaus that came to teach in Chicago, the staff was slowly supplemented by Americans. The method and aim of the school were likewise adapted to American requirements. Moholy-Nagy's successor at the head of the Institute of Design, Serge Chermayeff, however, remained quite true to the original Bauhaus, aiming at the education of the widely oriented universal thinker and designer. This changed step by step in the 1950s and through the merge with the Illinois Institute of Technology. The most radical alteration in the structure of the curriculum occurred after 1955 with the appointment of industry designer Jay Doblin, who placed a much stronger emphasis on economic applicability. The Institute of Design is even now still part of the Illinois Institute of Technology in Chicago, and rates as a respected and professionally oriented school of design.

The methods which came from the German Bauhaus and which were then transferred to Chicago and further developed there have been adopted in manifold modified form by other American schools. The Bauhaus is mainly responsible for the gradual reduction of the until then unchallenged predominance in the United States of the Beaux-Arts tradition.   PH

1 **László Moholy-Nagy** Title page "the new bauhaus", first school prospectus, 1937

2

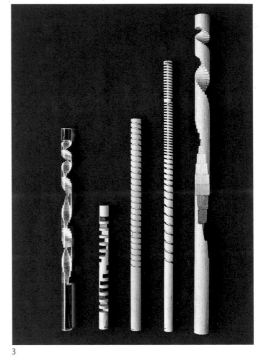

3

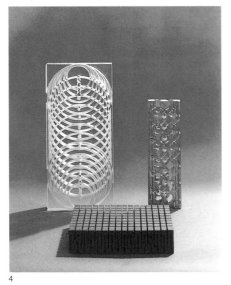

4

2 **Marie-Zoe Greene-Mercier**
Sculpture 1937/38
Polished bronze

3 **Richard Koppe**
Production pieces from Hin Bredendieck's preliminary course, 1937/38
Machine-cut wood and acrylic glass

4 **James Prestini**
Machine-worked production pieces in wood, aluminum, acrylic glass, originally 1940, reproduced in 1976

5

5 **Nathan Lerner**
Light box study,
1937
Photograph

6 **Students of the**
Institute of Design
Hand-sculptures,
1940's

6

Mies van der Rohe and Ludwig Hilberseimer at the Illinois Institute of Technology, 1938–1958

Mies van der Rohe was the second Bauhaus director after Walter Gropius to be appointed head of an American school of architecture. He was charged with the basic reform of the curriculum. In Chicago, Mies was confronted with the problem of adapting his ideas on studies of architecture and the rules of a large American university to a new concept. He had to find a compatibility between his rather anti-academic tendencies and the call for good results in a mass university.

His Bauhaus experience led him to devise a teaching plan divided into three phases. The first period was dedicated to the training of the hands and eyes in order to develop a feeling for proportion, structure, forms, and materials, their correlation and expression. The second period concentrated on the introduction to building materials and construction in order to comprehend the sensible and efficient correlation between materials, structure, and form. The last phase focused on an analysis of the purpose of a building as the fundament for both its design and the requirements of urban planning. Purpose was not confined to function: the studies underlined the differences between building types. The course ended with an introduction to artistic principles and problems in building.

Mies strongly influenced the school; he held that a building was developed rather than designed. The kernel of Mies' method was to create a balance between technical and artistic problems. Prerequisite was the perfect command of the skills of building craft. In line with his tuition in Germany, Mies expected his students to achieve more than a secure handling of elements from his own vocabulary; this provided the base for his course at IIT.

This emphasis on the artistic side of architecture distinguished the IIT curriculum from other American institutes of architecture, and most particularly from the course in Harvard, which had been developed by Walter Gropius and was based on the structural conditions of the building process, the outward appearance well embedded in conventional contemporary market tendencies.

This kind of tuition could only be successful if the other teachers thought exactly in the line of Mies. He was lucky enough to be able to enroll two teachers who had already worked with him at the Bauhaus: for the introductory courses he took on Walter Peterhans, who developed a class in "Visual Training" in order to support the training of mental and manual faculties required by Mies in the architecture course. Ludwig Hilberseimer took over the department for urban planning, for which he further developed ideas already expressed in Germany. These were then strongly imbued with American influence, leading his theories to expand to regional planning.

Mies van der Rohe's curriculum rapidly rose to fame and was often copied, not only in the USA. Worldwide, hardly any school of architecture could resist the attraction of his language of form.   CW

1 **Visual training with Walter Peterhans**
Space defined by different surfaces
Collage of papers with different structures on drawing board

2 **Urban planning with Ludwig Hilberseimer**
Study for the decentralization of Washington DC
Sprayed Indian ink and watercolor on drawing board

3 **Model from the construction course, second year**
Framework timber house on walled base
Wood, plywood, stone slabs

4 **Court house, fourth year**
Devised by Bruno Conterato, 1948
Indian ink drawing and collage on drawing board

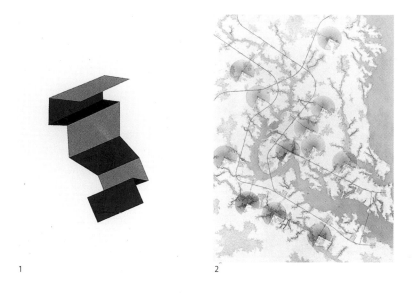

1

2

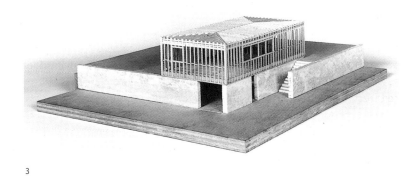

3

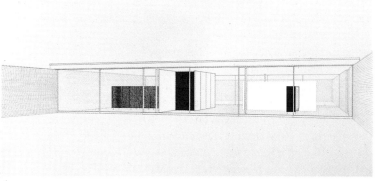

4

Hochschule für Gestaltung Ulm (Design School Ulm)

Founded in 1953, opened in 1955, and closed in 1968, the Hochschule für Gestaltung Ulm was continuously forced to position itself according to the Bauhaus. At first, the Bauhaus was considered to be a precursor, but later on, attempts were made to develop a new profile in order to disengage the school from its Bauhaus connotation.

Just as with the Bauhaus, the founding of the school was closely related to the spirit of the times. After the war, Inge Scholl, sister of the murdered opposition fighter Sophie Scholl from the circle of the White Rose, wanted to found a school for political and democratic education. Otl Aicher, later to become her husband, contributed to the planning and preparations. It was in talks with the sculptor Max Bill, however, that he succeeded in convincing them to alter the concept and found a school of design in the spirit of the Bauhaus. The founding was made possible by a generous donation provided by the American High Commissioner and intended to provide "instruction in the fields of civil responsibility, cultural productivity, and technical accomplishment". An additional aim in the deed of donation was "the improvement of quality, form, and functionality of commodities produced in Germany".

Max Bill remained the first rector for five years. He designed the school building and the houses for the teaching staff. Both building complexes are perfect models of the spirit of the Bauhaus director Hannes Meyer, and are highly praised in today's search for the roots of simple architecture.

At the time of Max Bill's departure from the school in 1957, which came after considerable and complex controversy, new priorities prevailed; the compulsory basic tuition, which had been taken over from the Bauhaus model, was done away with. Instead, an introduction specific to the first year of each course of study was elaborated. The courses offered were building, product design, visual communication, and photography and film.

From that point on, the pervasion of a theoretical rationalism into all fields of design became characteristic of the methodical approach. The Bauhaus had turned art into an inspirational partner for industry; Ulm did away with art altogether and called for a scientific approach. Max Bense, one of the teachers, spoke of "technical consciousness". Mathematics, statistics, psychology of perception, and semiotics were on the curriculum. These tendencies were checked only after Otl Aicher became director of the school in 1962.

Many of the products from Ulm were successful on the market; the new approach, for instance in the field of visual communication, is still in effect today. Otl Aicher designed the corporate identity for Lufthansa and ZdF (a TV channel), and left a visual mark on the Olympic Games of 1972 in Munich with his pictograms. In 1971, Herbert W. Kapitzki designed a color scheme information system for each level and department of the Historical Museum in Frankfurt am Main. The design for the Braun firm, the origins of which are closely related to the school in Ulm, is for many, even now, synonymous with "Ulm", and for years was exemplary for German design.

The Land of Baden-Württemberg closed the private school in 1968, when it was in an advanced state of dilapidation.   MD

1

1 **Max Bill**
Building complex of
the Design School
in Ulm, 1950–1955

2 **Hans Gugelot**
Radiogram combin-
ation SK4, 1956
Design for Braun
Co. Inc.

2

185

Bruno Adler
Das Weimarer Bauhaus
Darmstadt 1963

Werner Schütz
Der Staat als Mäzen
Darmstadt 1966

Nikolaus Pevsner
Fünfhundert Jahre
Künstlerausbildung
William Morris
Zwei Vorträge
Darmstadt 1966

Otto Stelzer
Erziehung durch
manuelles Tun
Darmstadt 1966

Hans Hildebrandt
Adolf Hölzel
Zeichnung – Farbe –
Abstraktion
Darmstadt 1969

**Walter Gropius
zum Gedenken**
Berlin 18. Mai 1883 –
Boston 5. Juli 1969
Darmstadt 1969

Walter Gropius
Bauten und Projekte
1906 bis 1969
Berlin, Zürich 1971
English Edition
Cambridge, Mass. 1972
Czech Edition, Prague 1972
Serbo-Croatian Edition,
Belgrad 1972
Corean Edition, Corea 1981

Paul Konrad Hoenich
Sonnenmalerei
Darmstadt 1971

Hannah Weitemeier
Licht-Visionen
Ein Experiment von
Moholy-Nagy
Berlin 1972

Hans M. Wingler
Bauhaus in America
Resonanz und Weiter-
entwicklung
Berlin 1972

Hans M. Wingler
Kleine Bauhaus-Fibel
Berlin 1974

Hans Heinz Stuckenschmidt
Musik am Bauhaus
Berlin 1976

Ein Museum für das Bauhaus?
Zur Eröffnung des nach
Plänen von Walter Gropius
errichteten Museumsgebäudes
am 1. Dezember 1979
Berlin 1979

Frei Otto
Chancen: Festrede zur Eröffnung des Museumsgebäudes
des Bauhaus-Archivs
Berlin 1979

Hans M. Wingler
Bauhaus-Archiv Berlin,
Museum für Gestaltung
Braunschweig 1979
English Edition
Braunschweig 1983

Bauhaus: Archiv, Museum
Sammlungskatalog
Architektur, Design, Malerei,
Graphik, Kunstpädagogik
Berlin 1981
2nd Edition Berlin 1984

Clark V. Poling
Kandinsky-Unterricht
am Bauhaus
Farbenseminar und analyti-
sches Zeichnen dargestellt am
Beispiel der Sammlung des
Bauhaus-Archivs Berlin
Weingarten 1982
Dutch Edition
Amsterdam 1983
English Edition
New York 1986

Reginald Isaacs
Gropius at/in Harvard
Berlin 1983

100 Jahre Walter Gropius
Schließung des Bauhauses
1933
Berlin 1983

Bauhaus Berlin
Auflösung Dessau 1932,
Schließung Berlin 1933,
Bauhäusler und Drittes Reich
Weingarten 1985

Vier Berliner Siedlungen der Weimarer Republik
Berlin 1987
Spanish Edition
Madrid 1992

Experiment Bauhaus
Das Bauhaus-Archiv, Berlin zu
Gast im Bauhaus Dessau
Berlin 1988
Japanese Edition
Tokyo 1995

Magdalena Droste
Bauhaus 1919–1933
Köln 1990
Translations in Engl., French,
Italian, Spanish, Portuguese,
Dutch, Danish, Finnish,
Swedish, Japanese

Ein Entwurf in eigener Sache
Bauhaus-Archiv,
Museum für Gestaltung
Berlin 1992

Sonja Günther
Wils Ebert, ein Bauhausschüler
1909–1979
Berlin 1993

Bauhaus-Moderne im Nationalsozialismus
Zwischen Anbiederung und
Verfolgung
München 1993

Bauhaus in Berlin
Bauten und Projekte
Berlin 1995

Bauhaus Archive
Exhibitions 1961–2005

(C) = Catalogue or Publication

Darmstadt

1. 4.–30. 4. 1961
Herbert Bayer
20 Aquarelle, Gouachen und
Zeichnungen

20. 8.–20. 9. 1961
Xanti Schawinsky
20 Gemälde und Zeichnungen

8. 5.–31. 5. 1962 (C)
Carl Fieger
Entwürfe und ausgeführte
Bauten
des Architekten

9. 11.–30. 11. 1962
Neuerwerbungen
Vorkursarbeiten, Möbel, Textilien, Tapeten

9. 11.–30. 11. 1962
Bildnerische Arbeiten
Werner Graeff, Jean Leppien,
Paul Reichle

8. 1.–30. 1. 1963
Rudolf Baschant
Zeichnungen und druckgrafische Arbeiten 1921–1954

8. 1.–30. 1. 1963 (C)
Ludwig Hirschfeld
Farbige Monotypien
1960–1962

30. 3.–26. 5. 1963 (C)
Arbeiten aus der graphischen Druckerei des Staatlichen Bauhauses in Weimar

18. 5.–23. 6. 1963 (C)
Walter Gropius
Werk und Persönlichkeit

3. 8.–25. 8. 1963
Georg Muche
Gemälde, Graphik, Zeichnungen

24. 3.–21. 4. 1964 (C)
Wandlungen bildnerischer Formelemente
Entwicklungsreihen aus
dem Werk von Eugen Batz
und Fritz Levedag

12. 4.–14. 6. 1964 (C)
Arbeiten aus der Weberei
des Bauhauses

4. 8.–21. 8. 1965
Shlomoh Ben David
Israel mit der Kamera erlebt

5. 11.–18. 12. 1966 (C)
Perspektive und Klang
Bildnerische Arbeiten von
Albert Flocon-Mentzel und
Henrik Neugeboren (Henri
Nouveau)

10. 2.–5. 3. 1967 (C)
Walter Peterhans
Elementarunterricht und
photographische Arbeiten

18. 11.–17. 12. 1967 (C)
Johannes Itten
Aquarelle und Zeichnungen

30. 11.–22. 12. 1968 (C)
Alfred Arndt
Maler und Architekt

28. 2.–27. 3. 1969 (C)
Fred Forbat:
Architekt und Stadtplaner

30. 5.–3. 7. 1969 (C)
Bauhäusler in Amerika:
Josef Albers – Farbgraphik
Walter H. Allner – Werbegraphik
Fritz Goro – Photographien

31. 1.–24. 3. 1970 (C)
Friedl Dicker, Franz Singer

30. 5.–5. 7. 1970 (C)
Walter Gropius
Das Spätwerk

14. 11. 1970–10. 1. 1971 (C)
Georg Muche
Das druckgraphische Werk

Berlin

23. 1.–14. 2. 1971 (C)
Walter Gropius
Bauten und Projekte 1906
bis 1969

18. 2.–30. 3. 1972 (C)
László Moholy-Nagy
Ausschnitte aus einem
Lebenswerk

10. 3.–29. 4. 1973
Georg Muche
Das druckgraphische Werk

19. 10.–2. 12. 1973 (C)
**Hannes Neuner und seine
Grundlehre**
Eine Weiterentwicklung des
Bauhaus-Vorkurses

22. 1.–21. 2. 1974 (C)
**100 Jahre Architektur
in Chicago**
Kontinuität und Struktur

22. 1.–21. 2. 1974 (C)
Nathan Lerner
Fotografie am New Bauhaus
1937–1945

8. 3.–21. 4. 1974 (C)
Johannes Itten
Der Unterricht

13. 9.–3. 11. 1974
Architekten am Bauhaus

13. 9.–3. 11. 1974
Oskar Schlemmer
»Der Mensch«

22. 11. 1974–12. 1. 1975 (C)
Herbert Bayer
Das druckgrafische Werk bis
1971

7. 3.–1. 6. 1975 (C)
Marcel Breuer
Architektur, Möbel, Design

18. 6.–24. 8. 1975 (C)
**Begegnungen mit
Menschen**
Das fotografische Werk von
Grete Stern

5. 9.–23. 11. 1975 (C)
Anni Albers
Bildweberei – Zeichnung –
Druckgrafik

5. 12. 1975–25. 1. 1976 (C)
Hubert Hoffmann
Architektur + Städtebau

20. 2.–4. 4. 1976 (C)
Benita Koch-Otte
Farblehre und Weberei

2. 9.–31. 10. 1976 (C)
Bauhäusler in Amerika

19. 11. 1976–30. 1. 1977 (C)
Kibbuz + Bauhaus
Arieh Sharon – der Weg
eines Architekten

19. 11. 1976–30. 1. 1977
Gunta Stadler-Stölzl
Wandteppiche

19. 11. 1976–30. 1. 1977
**50 Jahre Bauhaus-Gebäude
Dessau**

24. 2.–10. 4. 1977 (C)
György Kepes
Malerei, Fotografie, Light
Images, Druckgraphik

24. 2.–10. 4. 1977
Irena Blühová
Fotografien

17. 8. 1977–8. 1. 1978 (C)
**Kunstschulreform
1900 – 1933**

12. 4.–15. 5. 1978 (C)
Herbert Hirche
Architektur, Innenraum,
Design 1945–1978

24. 5.–25. 6. 1978 (C)
Alexander Rodtschenko
Fotografien 1920 –1938

21. 7.–4. 9. 1978 (C)
Ilja Tschaschnik

21. 7.–4. 9. 1978
Kunst und Technik

5. 5.–20. 7. 1980
**Der Barcelona-Pavillon
von Mies van der Rohe**

19. 9. 1980–12. 1. 1981 (C)
**Georg Muche – Sturm und
Bauhauszeit**
Das künstlerische Werk
1912–1927

18. 3.–8. 6. 1981 (C)
Ringl + Pit
Fotografien 1930–1933

18. 3.–8. 6. 1981 (C)
Kurt Kranz
Fotoreihen, Fotomontagen,
Fotos

3. 7.–13. 9. 1981 (C)
Bauhaus + Fotografie
Eugen Batz
Marta Hoepffner

2. 10.–29. 11. 1981 (C)
Stühle aus Stahl

15. 12. 1981–11. 4. 1982
El Muche
Zeichnungen

15. 12. 1981–11. 4. 1982
Gerhard Marcks
Grafik und Keramik

6. 5.–20. 6. 1982 (C)
Herbert Bayer
Das künstlerische Werk
1918 –1938

7. 7.–30. 9. 1982 (C)
Maximilian Debus
Bilder, Aquarelle, Zeichnun-
gen

1. 10.–30. 10. 1982
Hans Haffenrichter
Aquarelle, Zeichnungen,
Grafiken

1. 10.–30. 10. 1982
Mies van der Rohe
Architekturzeichnungen
vom Haus Werner

1. 11.–29. 11. 1982
Oswaldo Romberg
Farb-Environment

9. 12. 1982–23. 1. 1983 (C)
Ferdinand Kramer
Architektur und Design

9. 12. 1982–23. 1. 1983
Paul Citroen
Fotografien

10. 2.–17. 4. 1983 (C)
**Deutsche Kunst des
20. Jahrhunderts**
aus dem Busch-Reisinger
Museum der Harvard Uni-
versity, Cambridge, Mass.

5. 5.–12. 6. 1983 (C)
Georg Muche
Das malerische Werk
1928 –1982

24. 11. 1983–2. 1. 1984 (C)
Albert Flocon
Suites expérimentales

24. 11. 1983–2. 1. 1984 (C)
Katja Rose
Weberei am Bauhaus
1931–1933,
Bildwebereien 1964 –1983

11. 1.–19. 2. 1984 (C)
**Die Architektur Richard
Neutras**

9. 5.–15. 9. 1984
George Rickey
Freiplastiken

8. 8.–23. 9. 1984 (C)
Wassily Kandinsky
Russische Zeit und Bauhaus-
jahre 1915 –1933

24. 10. 1984–21. 1. 1985 (C)
**Siedlungen der zwanziger
Jahre – heute**
Vier Berliner Groß-
siedlungen 1924 –1984

6. 3.–14. 4. 1985 (C)
Almir Mavignier
Freie und angewandte
Arbeiten

Sommer 1985
Christoph Freimann
Plastik im Skulpturenhof
des Bauhaus-Archivs

5. 5.–7. 7. 1985 (C)
**Paul Klee als Zeichner
1921–1933**

18. 7.–15. 9. 1985 (C)
**Neue Museumsbauten in
der Bundesrepublik
Deutschland**

5. 10.–17. 11. 1985 (C)
Arbeiten mit/auf Papier
ars viva 85/86

16. 12. 1985–23. 2. 1986 (C)
Walter Gropius
Der Architekt

22. 3.–19. 5. 1986 (C)
Xanti Schawinsky
Malerei, Bühne,
Grafikdesign, Fotografie

5. 6.–31. 8. 1986 (C)
Gerhard Marcks
Zeichnungen und Aquarelle
aus der Bauhauszeit

15. 9.–2. 11. 1986 (C)
Herbert Bayer
Kunst und Design in
Amerika 1938–1985

13. 11. 1986–18. 1. 1987 (C)
Der vorbildliche Architekt
Mies van der Rohes
Architekturunterricht
1930 –1958 am Bauhaus
und in Chicago

4. 2.–26. 4. 1987 (C)
Gunta Stölzl
Weberei am Bauhaus und
aus eigener Werkstatt

4. 2.–26. 4. 1987 (C)
Hans Witwer
Flughafen-Restaurant
Halle-Leipzig 1929 –31

19. 5.–21. 6. 1987 (C)
L'Esprit nouveau
Le Corbusier und die
Industrie 1920 –1925

4. 7.–13. 9. 1987 (C)
Die Moral der Gegenstände
Hochschule für Gestaltung
Ulm

23. 9.–18. 10. 1987
**Braun Preis für
technisches Design**
Arbeiten der Preisträger

7. 11. 1987–10. 1. 1988 (C)
50 Jahre New Bauhaus
Bauhausnachfolge
in Chicago

20. 1.–17. 4. 1988 (C)
Täglich in der Hand
Industrieformen von
Wilhelm Wagenfeld

27. 4.–17. 7. 1988 (C)
**Wandel der
visuellen Kultur**
Gestaltung für
elektronische Medien

10. 8.–2. 10. 1988 (C)
Josef Albers
Eine Retrospektive

12. 10. 1988–15. 1. 1989 (C)
**Der Schrei nach
dem Turmhaus**
Der Ideenwettbewerb Hoch-
haus am Bahnhof Friedrichstraße Berlin 1921/22

31. 1.–27. 3. 1989 (C)
Experiment Bauhaus

31. 1.–27. 3. 1989 (C)
**Fotografien für
das Bauhaus**
Lucia Moholy –
Erich Consemüller

12. 4.–28. 5. 1989 (C)
Keramik und Bauhaus
Geschichte und Wirkungen
der keramischen Werkstatt
des Bauhauses

29. 9.–19. 11. 1989 (C)
Hannes Meyer
Architekt Urbanist Lehrer
1889 –1954

3. 2.–22. 4. 1990 (C)
Fotografie am Bauhaus
Überblick über eine
Periode der Fotografie
im 20. Jahrhundert

30. 5.–26. 8. 1990 (C)
Andor Weininger
Vom Bauhaus zur
konzeptuellen Kunst

19. 9. 1990–6. 1. 1991 (C)
Kurt Kranz
Das unendliche Bild

10. 4.–2. 6. 1991 (C)
Walter Dexel
Bild Zeichen Raum

3. 7.–30. 8. 1991 (C)
**Hannes Meyer und
Hans Wittwer**
Die Bundesschule des
ADGB in Bernau bei Berlin
1930 –1983

18. 8.–18. 11. 1991 (C)
Foto: Hinnerk Scheper
Ein Bauhäusler als
Bildjournalist in Dessau

27. 11. 1991–20. 1. 1992 (C)
**Objekt + Objektiv =
Objektivität?**
Fotografie an der HfG Ulm

9. 2.–3. 5. 1992 (C)
**Die Metallwerkstatt am
Bauhaus**

23. 5.–30. 8. 1992 (C)
Marcel Breuer
Design

6. 9.–11. 10. 1992 (C)
Potsdamer Platz
Wettbewerbsergebniss

16. 9.–31. 10. 1992
Rudolf Ortner
Architektur und Kunst

16. 9. 1992–3. 1. 1993
Roman Clemens
Bühnenbilder

17. 11. 1992–31. 1. 1993 (C)
Georg Muche
Gemälde, Zeichnungen,
Graphiken
Schenkungen an das
Bauhaus

17. 11. 1992–31. 1. 1993
Hein A. Molenaar
Zeichnungen aus dem
Unterricht Georg Muches
an der Itten-Schule Berlin

22. 2.–18. 4. 1993 (C)
Henry van de Velde
Ein europäischer Künstler
in seiner Zeit

28. 9.–28. 11. 1993 (C)
**Tel Aviv – Neues Bauen
1930–1939**
Fotografien von Irmel
Kamp-Bandau

8. 12. 1993–30. 1. 1994 (C)
Walter Peterhans
Fotografien 1927–1938

8. 12. 1993–30. 1. 1994 (C)
**Ringl + Pit: Grete Stern,
Ellen Auerbach**

27. 3.–29. 5. 1994 (C)
Adolf Meyer
Der zweite Mann

18. 6.–21. 8. 1994 (C)
Idee Farbe

29. 8.–6. 11. 1994
Fotografie am Bauhaus
100 ausgewählte Meister-
werke

27. 11. 1994–29. 1. 1995 (C)
**Das frühe Bauhaus und
Johannes Itten**

15. 2.–17. 4. 1995 (C)
Lucia Moholy
Bauhausfotografin

28. 4.–30. 7. 1995 (C)
**Ein Stück Großstadt
als Experiment**
Planungen am
Potsdamer Platz in Berlin

19. 8.–26. 11. 1995 (C)
**Das A und O des
Bauhauses**
Bauhauswerbung:
Schriftbilder, Drucksachen,
Ausstellungsdesign

19. 8.–26. 11. 1995 (C)
Werner David Feist
Fotografien am Bauhaus
1928 –30

25. 8.–3. 9. 1995
Bang & Olufsen
modern classics crafted for
the senses

7. 9.–12. 11. 1995 (C)
Alessi
Produkte aus der
Metallwerkstatt

22. 11. 1995–4. 2. 1996 (C)
Umbo
Vom Bauhaus zum
Bildjournalismus

14. 2.–1. 5. 1996 (C)
Bauhaus-Tapete
Reklame und Erfolg
einer Marke

15. 5.–18. 8. 1996 (C)
Auf den Spuren der Spuren
Gestalterischer Grundlagen-
unterricht heute

1. 9.–13. 10. 1996 (C)
Holographic network

3. 9.–3. 11. 1996 (C)
**Berliner Lebenswelten
der zwanziger Jahre**
Bilder einer untergegange-
nen Kultur photographiert
von Marta Huth

4. 12. 1996–23. 2. 1997 (C)
Das andere Bauhaus
Otto Bartning und die
Staatliche Bauhochschule
Weimar 1926 –1930

8. 3.–4. 5. 1997 (C)
wie wohnen?
Sieben Bauhaus-
einrichtungen

14. 5.–20. 7. 1997 (C)
Wohnen und Werkraum
Die Werkbundsiedlung
Breslau 1929

5. 8.–4. 10. 1997 (C)
Veltener Dinge
Keramik der zwanziger Jahre
aus den Steingutfabriken
Velten-Vordamm

24. 10.–23. 11. 1997 (C)
**Puls – Junges
Schwedisches Design**

11. 3.–1. 6. 1998 (C)
Andreas Feininger
Photographs 1928 –1988

20. 5.–1. 6. 1998
Das neue Berlin
Schülerfotowettbewerb

20. 5.–4. 10. 1998 (C)
Achim Pahle
Skulpturen im Garten

16. 6.–16. 8. 1998 (C)
Fagus
Industriekultur zwischen
Werkbund und Bauhaus

16. 9. 1998–5. 1. 1999 (C)
Das Bauhaus webt
Die Textilwerkstatt
des Bauhauses

31. 3. – 31. 5. 1999 (C)
**In der Vollendung liegt die
Schönheit**
Der Bauhaus-Meister Alfred
Arndt 1898 –1976

16. 6.–10. 10. 1999 (C)
Max Peiffer Watenphul
Ein Maler fotografiert Italien

9. 6.– 1. 8. 1999 (C)
Was nützt es?
Ein Museumsshop –
Design vom Bauhaus
bis heute

11. 8. – 10. 10. 1999 (C)
**Im Brennpunkt
der Moderne**
Mies van der Rohes
Haus Tugendhat

27. 10. 1999–27. 2. 2000 (C)
Punkt. Linie. Fläche.
Druckgraphik am Bauhaus
Zum 80. Gründungsjubiläum
des Bauhauses

15. 3.–1. 5. 2000 (C)
Kunst über dem Realen
Hans Thiemann und die
„Berliner Phantasten" 1946
Zum 90. Geburtstag des
Bauhauskünstlers

15. 3.–1. 5. 2000 (C)
Klaus Horstmann-Czech
Reliefobjekte

20. 5.–4. 6. 2000
In der Reihe Present Times
**Kommunikationsdesign
heute**
Projekte der Merz-Akademie
Stuttgart

20. 5.–19. 3. 2000
**Das logische Mittel zum
Zweck**
Hommage an den Werbe-
grafiker Herbert Bayer

10. 6.–23. 7. 2000
**Das Jahrhundert
der Architekten**

2. 8.–17. 9. 2000 (C)
Avantgarde im Dialog
Bauhaus, Dada und
Expressionismus in Japan

2. 8.–17. 9. 2000
Ann Holyoke Lehmann
Signs (1992)

27. 9.–26. 11. 2000 (C)
Tanaka Ikko
Graphik-Design aus Japan

27. 9.–27. 11. 2000
**Bauhaus-Architektur
in Dessau**
fotografiert von Stefan Kiess

1. 12. 2000–18. 1. 2001
**Dezemberaktion des
bauhaus-shops**
bauen spielen konstruieren
bauspiele und baukästen

6. 12. 2000–16. 4. 2001 (C)
Vorlesungswerkzeuge
Bildnerisches Gestalten
an der ETH, Zürich

3. 5. 2001–11. 3. 2002
Vision in Motion
Der Licht-Raum-Modulator
von Moholy-Nagy
Lichtstudien aus dem
New Bauhaus, Chicago

3. 5.–2. 7. 2001 (C)
FarbLichtSpiele
Der Bauhäusler
Ludwig Hirschfeld-Mack

17. 7.–15. 10. 2001 (C)
Friedl Dicker-Brandeis
Ein Leben für Kunst und
Lehre

26. 10. 2001–11. 4. 2002 (C)
Division as Structure
Zeichnungen und Reliefs
von Paul Mason

26. 10. 2001–11. 3. 2002 (C)
Mehr als der bloße Zweck
Mies van der Rohe
am Bauhaus 1930–1933

14. 4.–2. 6. 2002 (C)
extrakt
Junge Schmuckdesigner in
Deutschland

12. 6.–2. 9. 2002 (C)
Montessori
Lehrmaterialien
1931 bis 1935,
Möbel und Architektur

26. 10. 2002–10. 3. 2003 (C)
Bauhaus-Möbel
Eine Legende wird
besichtigt

16. 4.–30. 6. 2003 (C)
**bauhausleuchten?
KANDEMLICHT!**
Die Zusammenarbeit des
Bauhauses mit der Leipziger
Firma Kandem

16. 7.–15. 9. 2003 (C)
Der Bau einer neuen Welt
Architektonische Visionen
des Expressionismus

1. 10.–30. 11. 2003 (C)
**Licht - Bewegung - Zahl -
Raum**
Die Grundlehre von
Werner Schriefers
Wuppertal 1949–1965

10. 12. 2003–9. 2. 2004 (C)
**Hommage an
Philip Rosenthal**

4. 2.–19. 9. 2004
New Bauhaus Chicago

25. 2.–6. 6. 2004 (C)
Elsa Thiemann: Fotografin
Bauhaus und Berlin

16. 6.–24. 10. 2004
Der Afrikanische Stuhl
Meisterwerk des Bauhauses
entdeckt!

27. 10. 2004–9. 1. 2005 (C)
**Happy Birthday!
Bauhaus-Geschenke**
Eine Ausstellung zum
25. Jubiläum des Bauhaus-
Archivs am Tiergarten

29. 1.–16. 5. 2005 (C)
**Egon Eiermann
(1904–1970)**
Die Kontinuität der Moderne

8. 6.–12. 9. 2005 (C)
Farbenfroh!
Die Werkstatt für
Wandmalerei am Bauhaus

12. 10. 2005–9. 1. 2006 (C)
Tempo, Tempo!
Bauhaus Fotomontagen von
Marianne Brandt

20. 1.–20. 3. 2006 (C)
Alma Siedhoff-Buscher
Eine neue Welt für Kinder

5. 4.–5. 6. 2006 (C)
Günter Kupetz
Industrial Designer

21. 6.–4. 9. 2006 (C)
Color in Transparency
Farbfotoexperimente von
László Moholy-Nagy,
1934–1946

26. 7.–4. 9. 2006
Mies Memory Box

20. 9.–20. 11. 2006 (C)
**Kazuyo Sejima +
Ryue Nishizawa SANAA**

6. 12. 2006–5. 2. 2007 (C)
Schenkung Dora Hartwig

193

The collection of the Bauhaus Archive in overview

1. Art and education

The Bauhaus Archive has a substantial collection of paintings, drawings and sculptures by the masters and students of the Bauhaus and includes works by Albers, Feininger, Itten, Klee, Kandinsky, Muche, Moholy-Nagy, Schlemmer, and Schreyer. Important work groups of single artists have reached the collection in the form of legacies, endowments or permanent loans, including, for example, a major part of the artistic work of Georg Muche, the artistic estate of Lothar Schreyer, the paintings of the student Hans Thiemann, and the graphic design work of Herbert Bayer.

The graphic collection has now evolved to a holding of more than 8,500 sheets. It includes drawings, watercolors, and other works on paper, as well as engravings by masters and students of the Bauhaus. Above all, it comprises the complete and worldwide unique series of graphic cycles and portfolios from the Weimar period by Feininger, Kandinsky, Marcks, Moholy-Nagy, Muche, and Schlemmer, as well as the complete Bauhaus prints from the series "Neue Europäische Graphik" ("New European Graphics"). In addition, many artists are represented with samples of their work from before or after the Bauhaus period. Kandinsky, for instance, with some of his early woodcuts, Albers and Muche with individual prints and series of engravings from the thirties until the sixties.

The graphic collection also includes commercial work – posters and other printed materials, designs for advertising and lettering etc. – as well as a rich choice of materials from the different courses at the Bauhaus: from the preliminary courses by Itten, Muche, Moholy-Nagy, and Albers, as well as from the courses given by Kandinsky, Klee, Schmidt, Schlemmer, and Schreyer. The history leading up to the Bauhaus is documented with drawings by Adolf Hölzel, with a compilation of studies by his pupil Lily Hildebrandt at the Art Academy in Stuttgart, and with several works of 1902–12 by Maria Strakosch-Giesler, a Kandinsky student in Munich. The Bauhaus succession is documented through works by students of the New Bauhaus and of the Hochschule für Gestaltung in Ulm (Design School).

2. Workshop production and industrial design

The collection encompasses products from all the workshops throughout the various phases of the Bauhaus: from handmade individual pieces and prototypes to examples of industrial fabrication in series. The extensive holdings in furniture, lamps, works in metal, and ceramics, the rich group of works from the Bauhaus textile workshop, together with a profusion of fabric designs and samples are of particular interest. Exemplary objects from the workshops and industrial production of the institutions succeeding the Bauhaus – the Staatliche Bauhochschule in Weimar (State School for Architecture), the New Bauhaus and the Hochschule für Gestaltung in Ulm (Design School) – represent later developments.

3. Architecture collection

200 works from the courses at the Bauhaus comprise the center of the architecture collection. This extensive holding focuses particularly on all related fields during the period under Mies van der Rohe, from technical education to training in three-dimensional thought based on the study of floor plans, to interior decoration.

The architecture of Walter Gropius is present in a small but very rich selection of drawings and architect's copies and in a complete photographic documentation. Access to the estate of his long standing partner Adolf Meyer enabled the divided photographic records to be reunited. The archive of the Fagus-Werk (Fagus factory) represents a quite unique collection of some 700 architect's copies together with an extensive photographic documentation of products and building projects, including the exemplary series by Albert Renger-Patzsch, together with appx. 300 files compiling materials from all areas of activity. In addition, the Bauhaus Archive maintains the estates of following architects:

Wils Ebert (appx. 1,300 plans, numerous sketches, source material, correspondence, and photographic archive from the years 1928–79) Helmut Heide (appx. 600 drawings and architect's copies, photographic documentation from 1932 until the eighties) Gustav Hassenpflug (complete photographic documentation of his work 1927–68) Fritz Kaldenbach (124 drawings and architect's copies 1906–18) Karl Keller (1,800 drawings and architect's copies from the twenties and the thirties, partly from the Bauhochschule Weimar (School for Architecture) under Erich Dieckmann) Franz Singer (appx. 800 drawings and architect's copies 1921–50, photographic documentation of his work in Vienna) Hans Soeder (appx. 600 drawings, architect's copies, sketches and photographs from his entire period of production 1917–60) Philipp Tolziner (appx. 200 plans and extensive documentary materials from his time in the Soviet Union)

In all, the collection comprises at the present some 8,000 sheets and a row of architectural models. The most prominent piece is the model of the Bauhaus building in Dessau from 1925 which Walter Gropius had carefully kept until it could be integrated in the collection.

4. Collection of documents

One of the central aims of the Bauhaus Archive as postulated at the time of its founding in 1960 was the preservation of "all documents related to the activities and the cultural heritage of the Bauhaus". Since then, individual collections from over 500 teachers and students have been gathered, as well as others concerning personalities and institutions related to the ideas and history of the Bauhaus, i e. to the Bauhaus succession in the USA and to various reformed art schools in Germany. The history of the Hochschule für Gestaltung in Ulm (Design School) is documented, thanks to a section of the archive from the school as it was at its dissolution in 1968.

The collection covers letters, manuscripts, and other written documents, as well as printed materials. The archive now has access to more than 3,000 file units, themselves composed of numerous individual sheets. In addition, it boasts a library of all Bauhaus publications, including a collection of trade publications and sales catalogues from diverse fields of industrial design, principally from the twenties and thirties.

Walter Gropius' readiness to transfer his extensive private archive covering the history of the Bauhaus in Weimar and Dessau is of major importance. Even today, it constitutes the indispensable core of the collection of documents. This includes materials from the pre-Bauhaus history, its foundation, detailed documentation of the political discussion concerning the school, part of the minutes of the board of masters from the years 1919–1923, as well as valuable records on everyday life at the school, such as official contracts, the curriculum, statutes and programs. Many manuscripts provide an insight in the manifold publication, lecture, and teaching activities of Gropius during and following his time at the Bauhaus. A collection of press cuttings from 1917–1934 offers information on the public impact of the Bauhaus and of Gropius'

architecture. In addition, we have his correspondence from 1910–1969, with over 1,000 addressees, among them Marcel Breuer, Max Bill, Theo van Doesburg, Albert Einstein, Lyonel Feininger, Theodor Heuss, Le Corbusier, László Moholy-Nagy, Ludwig Mies van der Rohe, Erwin Piscator, Hans Scharoun, Kurt Schwitters, Kenzo Tange, Henry van de Velde, and Frank Lloyd Wright. The archive also includes an important quantity of letters from his wife, Alma Mahler-Gropius.

The transfer of the Gropius estate was followed by numerous donations and contributions by other former members of the Bauhaus or their relatives, but also by donations of materials from others who stood close to the Bauhaus, such as Hans Maria Wingler, the founding director of the Bauhaus Archive. During the past years, the collection was enlarged through acquisitions, such as part of the estate of the art critic Adolf Behne, who was a close friend of Walter Gropius. The following list compiles only the most important estates and partial estates, with their relating dates and sizes:

Walter Gropius, 1903 – 69, appx. 46,000 sheets
Georg Muche, 1919– 82, appx. 10,000 sheets
Roman Clemens 1919 –31, 1950–92, appx. 600 sheets
Hans Thiemann, 1931–79, appx. 3,000 sheets
Philipp Tolziner, 1931– 95, appx. 22,000 sheets
Lucia Moholy, 1933– 86, appx. 19,000 sheets
Adolf Behne, 1912 –34, correspondence 150 sheets, printed materials 400 sheets
Paul Vogler, 1929 – 52, appx. 800 sheets
Hans M. Wingler, 1911– 84, appx. 6,000 sheets

5. Collection of artistic photography

The epicenter of the collection of artistic photography from members of the Bauhaus consists in the works of the great stimulators and teachers Lucia Moholy, László Moholy-Nagy, and Walter Peterhans. Their work – predominantly from the twenties and thirties – is exemplary for all kinds of photographic expression of that time: experiment and snapshot, composition and portrait, object and architecture photography.

In all, the collection comprises 5,000 prints (divided into appx. 4,000 vintage prints and 1,000 modern prints) by 117 artists from the Bauhaus, its radius and succession. It also includes some 1,500 original negatives of works by Lucia Moholy, Herbert Schürmann, and Eugen Batz, the largest portion of which is constituted by the estate of Lucia Moholy with her documentation of the buildings and products of the Bauhaus. Smaller, high-quality groupings contain works by Herbert Bayer, Marianne Brandt, and Erich Consemüller. The Feininger family is united in the photographic collection with photographs by Lyonel Feininger, as well as by his sons Andreas and T. Lux Feininger. The collection also includes the only extensive documentation of the class of Walter Peterhans at the Dessau Bauhaus, with works by 23 photographers, among them and principally Herbert Schürmann and Eugen Batz. And the Bauhaus Archive owns a collection unique in Europe of some 500 photos from the New Bauhaus, including shots by György Kepes, Nathan Lerner, and Henry Holmes Smith.

6. Photo archive

This unparalleled photo archive on the history of the Bauhaus, its people, workshops and production has become an indispensable partner for research and publishing houses around the world. At the moment, it comprises appx. 50,000 photos – half originals and half reproductions – and more than 1,500 ektachromes. Central themes are portraits, views of works created in the courses and the workshops, Bauhaus and Bauhaus-related architecture and design, and finally shots of the artefacts in the collection of the Bauhaus Archive.

Here again, 4,000 photos on the work and person of Walter Gropius stand out. Further extensive fields of the collection are image documents on the life and work of Josef Albers, Herbert Bayer, Marianne Brandt, Marcel Breuer, Adolf Meyer, Hannes Meyer, Ludwig Mies van der Rohe, László Moholy-Nagy, Georg Muche, Oskar Schlemmer, Joost Schmidt, Franz Singer, and Hans Thiemann. In addition, the documentation covers everyday life at the Bauhaus, the workshops and the studios, the legendary Bauhaus parties, the Bauhaus stage, architecture and exhibition design of the twenties, as well as the New Bauhaus.

7. Library

The library, comprising 22,000 volumes, is accessible to everyone. The specialized collection provides literature on the Bauhaus, its context, and the artists, architects, and designers involved. In addition, the documentation extends to art, architecture, photography, and design of the twentieth century, with a main focus on the twenties, and includes a rich selection of historical and contemporary architecture and design magazines.

Services and map

Guided tours in the permanent collection and temporary exhibitions are available on advance reservation to groups up to 25 persons. Please phone +49 30 25 40 02 43

When available, the lecture room can be used for special events, training programs, and lectures. Reservation fee on arrangement. For further information phone +49 30 25 40 02 43

Bauhaus Archive Berlin
Museum für Gestaltung
Klingelhöferstraße 14, D-10785 Berlin
Telephone: +49 30 25 40 02 0
Infoline: +49 30 25 40 02 78
Facsimile: +49 30 25 40 02 10
e-mail: bauhaus@bauhaus.de
Internet: http://www.bauhaus.de

The Museum is open daily except Tuesday
10 am– 5 pm
The Library is open Monday to Friday
9 am– 1 pm

Access by public transport:
U-Bahn Nollendorfplatz
Bus 100, 187, 343 and M29 Lützowplatz

Coffee Shop in the Bauhaus Archive
Open daily except Tuesday 10 am   5 pm
Telephone: +49 30 25 40 02 62

Members of the Bauhaus Archive e.V. (non-profit association) are provided with a Bauhaus Archive Service Card. They automatically receive invitations to the exhibition openings, have free admission to all exhibitions, and are entitled to reduced prices on the items sold in the Bauhaus Shop.
The association is exclusively and immediately a non-profit organization, serving cultural, scientific, and educational purposes. The yearly member fee represents a substantial support to the Museum. Corporate membership is also possible.

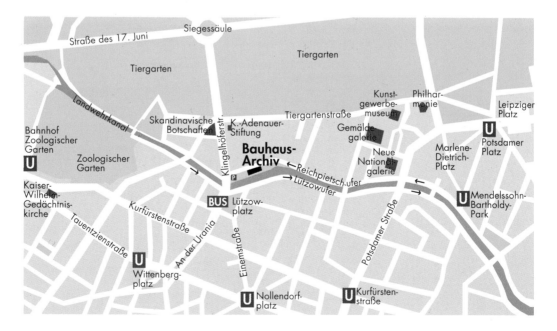

Index

Photo credits

All photographs Bauhaus Archive Berlin except for:
Pl. 4, p.18: Musée national d'art moderne/Centre Georges Pompidou, Paris, legs Nina Kandinsky

Photographers, if not already mentioned in the captions:
Markus Hawlik, Gunter Lepkowski, Atelier Schneider, Fotostudio Bartsch, Reinhard Friedrich, Hermann Kiessling, Berlin